The Lotus Project

the art of being a woman

&

alluring well being and beauty through green living

by

Lyn Hicks

The Lotus Project

the art of being a woman

&

alluring well being and beauty through green living

by

Lyn Hicks

THE **Difference** PRESS

THE LOTUS PROJECT
The Art of Being A Woman

‚

Alluring Well Being and Beauty
Through Green Living

by
Lyn Hicks

©2013 Lyn Hicks

Published by The Difference Press, Washington DC

The Difference Press, and the wax seal design are registered trademarks of Becoming Journey, LLC

ISBN: 978-1-936984-15-2

Library of Congress Control Number: 2013933684

Cover design by: Drai Bearwomyn

Interior design by Karen Leigh Burton, Poodles Doodles

Photography provided by: Terree Yeagle, The Moment Photography

Lyn Hicks

Dedication

I dedicate this book to all those who have shared knowledge that has helped me to learn about myself. I have had so many teachers in the school of life, from old wisdom to enemies who taught me great lessons in self-awareness. I especially thank the women—teachers, friends, and mentors in the great chain of women—who have been so instrumental in my journey. I give honor to those courageous women who came before me in my ancestral line and around the world, and to all those who share their knowledge with us in the hopes that we may brighten our light!

Table of Contents

Lyn Hicks

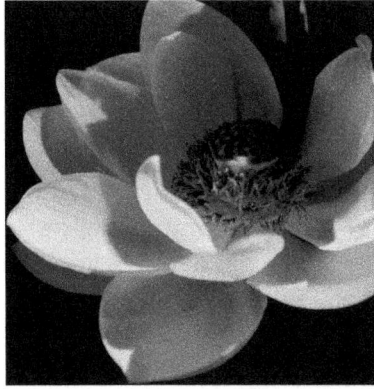

Foreword
To Be a Garden Goddess!

I loved when my friend Donna gave me that sign for my birthday! It rang so deep for me! To honor my femininity as a sacred gift, a wonder. We are all goddesses, princesses, lovely queens! A smile creeps in when we just picture such an image.

When we were young we wanted to be Cinderella, transformed into beauty from our everyday lives and honored in all our femininity. Cleopatra, Venus, Aphrodite and Isis also come to mind—beautiful, brilliant women capable of doing all and ruling wisely with joy and power.

We don't have many recent role models of this; they are either powerful, masculine-looking women or extremely sensual, sexual women. There are, however, many strong and beautiful women in the old societies who represent the feminine power that inspires us to accept femininity as a gift, to view beauty as a power, and to embrace our "feeling" nature.

Vibrationally we don't know how it feels to be full of ourselves in both beauty and power. Vibration is movement. It's an emotional feeling; emotion is energy in motion. It is not thinking or words but a vibration, an emotional state. Vibing in ease, beauty and grace, joyfully, effortlessly, smiling and pleasurably alive—this is how feminine power moves.

She is safe, she is open and playful; she achieves things with pleasure at a melodic, rhythmic pace. She is happy and enjoys her work in life. Beautiful and sophisticated in her power and magnificence, she tends and befriends the world. She is a warrior and a beauty, soft and strong, much like Mother Nature—a creator and collaborator with all! This is Shakti power in the East. It is magnetizing and beautiful. It is the state women should be operating in and we are not.

The world has given us many messages contrary to this thinking. Beauty has become an outward quality that is created by manipulative and unnatural procedures. Women in power often appear or act masculine, joining the world of competition and survival of the fittest. The "I am better than you/smarter than you/prettier than you" mindset creates cliques, judgment and antagonism in our feminine culture.

We are victims in so many ways, often of each other. It is not easy to embrace our femininity, to love being female in this world where masculine power rules. Yet a shift is coming about. Women are gathering and wondering how to thrive in a different way, not sure what it is but knowing that owning their femininity is part of the journey. Feeling "less than" has taken its toll. Embracing our emotional way of being, our intuitive nature, equal in power to the thinking way of men, I am part of the movement that brings back this feminine way! I want to embody the sacredness of women.

We need to create a new structure for women (and the world at large) where there is a stronger feminine community that supports this graceful and powerful way. We are good communicators, flexible at accepting situations and open to ways of improvement. We are great students, ready to seek collaborative solutions, developing the ability to move through life feeling its depths—not controlled by our emotions but using our power to harness the energy of those emotions and direct it into a path of talent that fulfills us.

We have these great qualities that are not being developed and used in the ways that would bring more joy and ease into our lives. Our vibrational life energy is on a deep feeling level. It is not strategic thinking or logic that rules us. We move opposite the way men move, complementary to their process, equal in value but very different in our approach and what we offer the world.

I offer this book to help you see the shift in thinking that occurs when our emotional nature is in power within us. To make choices based on feeling, not relying on logic or efficiency. The shift is in honoring yourself and the things around you, expanding into a deeper feeling of why and how you move, heart-driven. When we make choices that come from that space, they are empowering and loving, there is energy behind them, and they have the support of the universe because they are for the good of all.

A woman moves in an emotional way, considering much more than just her own wellness. Everyday choices can become yoga practices, processes of nurturing and loving. That is how I want to live—as an artist of creative living, acting purposefully with an awakened heart, gracefully moving in joy and helping the world. Not fighting or competing to survive, or rushing about in an anxious state.

Our emotions are powerful energy! Used wisely they offer a different power than the mind. Moving with emotion is the gift of femininity, nurturing so that all may thrive in a more connected world. A more relaxed way of creating! This is the deeper meaning of the green movement, which is so connected to the feminine way: knowing that nurturing all toward wellness and harmony is the gift of femininity. It should not be a struggle. We can make it a pleasure by adding a woman's touch!!!!

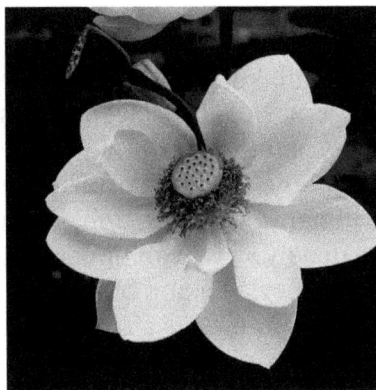

CHAPTER ONE
An Awakening of Feminine Spirit!

Each of us is a Lotus Project. We land in this world, surrounded by the water of our family ponds, drawing power from the sun of youthful energy, nourished by the rich mud of our experiences. We are raised in our home environments, developing all kinds of habits, attachments and patterns as we explore life, only to find as we grow that we have been programmed away from ourselves.

The moment we realize that we have been doing what we think is expected of us and that our bright light is not being fed, we can begin to rise from the muck and mire, to shoot up our stems and start again the journey towards flowering into the wonderful beings we were meant to be. We can uncover our essence and purpose, our gifts and talents that somehow never made it out into the world.

As children we jumped to so many naïve conclusions, closing off parts of ourselves for protection from some comment or situation. Now we can see the bright hidden gem within us and begin to cultivate and share it. All human beings go through this journey, seeking the true self by peeling away the onion-like layers that have grown tightly around it. As women we must uncover our hidden depths by nourishing ourselves on many levels.

With this book, I share my story to encourage you to bring vitality, wellness and magic back into your life by reconsidering the ways you live. I want you to be open to the wellness and healing offered by the nurturing aspect of the modern green movement. Not only to save the Earth but to embrace your deeper nature as a creator, to connect with your brilliance so you can overflow into the world.

Women are the flowers of humanity and we provide its fruits. When we naturally nourish ourselves on all levels, we will positively impact our families, our communities and the Earth. A great awakening is occurring that has to do with women, the feminine principle and the essence of our feminine energy that will harmonize our global community. We need to tap into ourselves more deeply so we can understand what it is we all need in this next cycle of the journey. Seeking true nourishment and nurturing begins with ourselves and continues as a recurring theme through all areas of our lives.

The Circle of Women

There has been a women's movement growing my whole life! Each stage of it seems to get deeper and deeper, allowing women the freedom of enjoying life to the fullest on their terms. It has not come without much work and courage! I like being a woman; our process is transforming so wonderfully at this time. We are learning to understand our bodies, our creativity that comes from sexual energy, our true beauty within and without. I support the women's movement and the honoring of our feminine essence—creative, inspiring, flexible and changing like nature. We are the gems and founts of human creation, nurturing it as the Earth nurtures all life.

Over time, great wisdom about our sexual energy, our magnetism, our creative energy, and our allure has been lost and we view sexual energy only as the power to attract a man and attach to him. This is such small thinking; it is no wonder we find ourselves worn out, dissatisfied and yearning.

But we are awakening, learning to use this creative energy in all our undertakings! It is the energy of life. Nature, the great creator, uses this energy in all ways. We too need to learn to use this for all our endeavors, not only for men. Learning about the many aspects of our sexual, creative energy is an essential life lesson for our time on Earth. We need to strengthen the feminine culture to overcome our society's misunderstanding, misuse, and abuse of this positive power.

Our current thinking on sex, sexual energy, and seduction has degraded women and our power to manifest. Like nature, the great creator, women also use sexual energy to design and bring forth life—not only children but all our creations. It awakens our individuality, our hearts, our truths, our focus and our connection to others. It is a deeper understanding women need to own and activate within themselves to balance the world that so needs our collaborative way!

We are overwhelming ourselves in a competitive system of adrenaline. We need to be in oxytocin, it is our hormone, activating the parasympathetic nervous system, inspiring us to tend and befriend. We are collaborators, communicators, conflict solvers and inspiring forces. These are the divine feminine qualities needed at this time in our world. The emerging feminine culture helps us reattach to this essence.

This is our movement to clear up so many of the beliefs and fears that have created a disconnection, a miseducation about ourselves, our beauty, our magnetism, our dynamic way. I choose to promote the revival of the Red Tent, a strong community, a collaboration of women working together, building themselves and overflowing this energy into the community. There is great information about these transformations worldwide. Expand your field, your influence, learning and connection.

I have chosen to learn the practices to transform my own understanding of feminine essence. Doing so naturally changes you, allowing your power to unfold for you in your life as an individual, exquisite and unique. It is a lovely process and I invite you to engage in it!

The Art of Honoring

A great many of us have heard that we need to honor ourselves, but how? What does that mean? How can we move through all of our challenging tasks and fit in the time to nourish ourselves?

We must cultivate awareness of a deeper level of existence and perception. Be open to new ideas and ways of living. It is time to put attention on ourselves, experiencing rather than thinking, activating our feeling nature, doing something that nurtures us on many levels. We have been living in our heads, learning about the mind, copying the masculine way of learning and doing. We need to move into health and vitality by making our living more meaningful in all phases, by adding conscious awareness to our daily tasks and chores so that we become artists painting a joyful life rather than runners racing to its finish.

The chapters that follow offer shifts in perspective on your tasks of family caring, ways to involve your heart, body and spirit in the choices you make to nourish yourself and others. This is the tale of my journey toward green living for myself and my family, becoming connected to all the levels of my being and aligning them.

It all begins with honoring myself. Each choice brings me back to doing what is right in my heart, right for myself, and right for others. Living curiously, seeing things as new and interesting, having an open mind and a student's perspective—these are gifts that women naturally have. We love to switch things up, and this allows us to be more present and perceptive. We need to get back to feeling ourselves and moving in a relaxed way! There are many parts of ourselves awaiting discovery and we are in the midst of a great awakening of those deeper levels of spirit!

Green choices are choices for wellness and healing, ways to live that harmonize body, mind and spirit. We begin by learning to fuel ourselves with the right information about what we put in, on and around us. Be open to new ways. Transformation is all around. It is our time to flower!

Chapter Two
Nourish Yourself Wisely

When I look back to see where this whole health and wellness lifestyle began in my life, I would have to say it came with motherhood. I did not consciously plan to be a mother—most things I do aren't conventional. The path just doesn't unwind the so-called "correct" way for most of us although we seem to think that if we follow some path we have been trained for, we will find happiness. This transformation we are taking part in is about uncovering who we are, not who we think we should be.

When my precious daughter Erika was born, I realized what it was like to really care for someone else's life. It was a huge discovery. I was the first of my friends to step into motherhood and I took it very seriously because you have to. Caring for another without really understanding how to care for myself was a crucial growth point for me.

Erika was a colicky baby at first. We discovered that she couldn't digest standard formula well and breastfeeding didn't work for us beyond six weeks. It was a challenging way to begin, an intense start to motherhood. We finally found a formula she could digest and things changed—what a relief for us to be able to enjoy each other without her crying from pain! When it came time to feed her solids, she could not digest the preservatives in baby food. I had to make my own by grinding fresh food for her. Let me tell you, I was not into this process! But it was necessary so I did it. I needed to increase my understanding of food and nourishment to make life bearable for Erika and for myself.

My friend Beth told me about *Prevention* magazine and how it educated her about health and wellness. I got a subscription and the learning began. I am not inspired by cooking so I looked into foods and found that broccoli, cantaloupe and berries are some of the best things we can eat. I searched for knowledge about how to feed my daughter and husband the most nutritious foods. This is where I began to view health and wellness from a preventative standpoint. I learned how important it is to feed yourself well so your body can operate at its best.

Our journey is ongoing as we learn more about our bodies and all the levels we operate on. The physical level is the first, and nutrition is tied to the performance of our physical bodies. It is here you must begin your journey. *Prevention* also dealt with other levels, offering practices like yoga, breathing and movement to promote mental and emotional health— other aspects of the health of our whole beings. In the great school of womanhood, this knowledge is Self Care 101.

This magazine also showed me why organic food is worth more money and why you should choose it for yourself and your family. Chemical residue is all around us, at home and at work, in our furnishings, cleaners, personal products, and foods. Eating nutritious organic food to build and protect our bodies just makes practical sense from a health standpoint.

We were a single-income household in expensive Bucks County so we didn't have much money. Spending money on food seemed like a good use of resources for my family. *Prevention* opened me up to a new way of thinking about my role at home. I read to educate myself in order to become the *nourisher* of my home and family. We have not been educated well enough on nutrition. The food we feed our families and the environments we create for them can nourish or slowly kill them. I took this very seriously knowing that it was on my head.

Because I was chunky growing up, I wanted to teach my daughter good nutrition so she would never have weight issues. And in case she did, I wanted to share with her ways to get back in control, to overcome the sense of lack that can come with being overweight. I wanted to cure her and myself of the unhealthy relationship to food we inherited from our ancestors.

Eating for Energy

We are designed to eat in order to get the energy we need to do our tasks, yet most of us haven't felt hunger in years. We don't notice when we are truly hungry; we eat because we feel low emotionally or because we are gathered with others. Our eating has little to do with energy management. We have lost touch with the digestive system, which is an energy management system designed to fuel the operation of our bodies.

We are far off the mark when it comes to food. It is time for an important shift in wellness; weight problems have become a national epidemic. Gluttonous, unhealthy eating is not nourishing. Our physical bodies can't operate well on emotion-based eating.

Our second chakra, Svadhisthana is located in the womb and relates to our sense of taste. When we don't approach life with creativity and are not inspired artfully, we naturally reach for food for pleasure. When we are not fulfilling our creative desires, we often turn to food for sensual pleasure and overindulge. Taking a step back, noticing this, and bringing our creativity to better food preparation is one way to use this desire in health and vitality.

Creativity is so important to life, and its imbalance shows up often in food consumption. This is an important shift you need to make if you want more vital energy. Educating yourself on nutrition and why eating organic is a choice for health. There are many information sources out there and you can make feeding yourself and family an art—a creative expression unique to you, your needs and your family's needs.

This was my start to true green living. It was the beginning of my ongoing study of health, beauty and wellness. It's important to have your engine run clean, to know that food is about giving you fuel to do what you need to do. It is wonderful to eat large when you are with others. We gather with our families around food, but we are nourished on many levels. It isn't about the food, it's about the camaraderie, support and love. We take in the food to ritualize it and bring that love into our bodies.

This is fine on occasion, but eating unconsciously and emotionally actually harms our well-being. Trying to nourish our hearts with food is clogging them. We each need to learn how to do this best for our family. There is no magic formula or certain way; it is about finding balance for your family. This is part of the life journey to conscious nourishment. Watch yourself and your patterns of eating—it will be very telling.

So the journey to health that supports your spirit begins with your eating. It's how you start getting yourself as healthy as you can in relation to your food, your heart and your mind. Lousy food creates low emotional states and negative thinking. Good food does just the opposite. Poor eating can cause depression, low energy, and lethargy. These states may have nothing to do with your life and current conditions; they can be caused entirely by low quality food. Take on your nourishing role proudly and really sink into it. This will transform you. It is the first plane of learning, putting your body and health first because it matters in everything you do. You will attain so much more in all areas of your life as you begin to understand your body's need for nourishment and your role in providing it.

You must begin with yourself. Learn to nourish yourself wisely—diets and crazy fads are not the way. Approach nourishment from this perspective will enable you to feed yourself and others without spending all your time thinking about eating and working out. There is so much information out there that is too complicated. I offer some great thoughts, but just knowing that you are eating to fuel yourself is a great perspective to set you up. Then you will have more brain space to focus on the important things in life. It is your responsibility to support health in yourself, your family, and the greater community. This will empower you!

All of this learning led to another step in my green living journey—joining a CSA (community-supported agriculture) farm. Getting nutrient-rich organic food from your own community is a wonderful start. Grown out of local earth and the hearts of your neighbors, grown to nourish your body, it is way deeper than just the good tomatoes. It is a whole new set of actions and processes that link you with your community, your food and health.

I learned so much about new foods and seasonal eating, and I developed a greater appreciation for energy-producing foods. CSA helps make eating a meditation from the field to our tables, consciously honoring the art of feeding ourselves. The whole process is different from grocery store shopping. You know that great feeling you get when you stop by a farm stand to grab a few things. It is a deeply emotional choice that has to do with greater honoring of yourself and what you use to fuel you.

The art of cooking with nourishing thoughts, vibrant colors, and quality food makes the cooking process creative and joyous. We need to return to this type of thinking. Your body will naturally balance and reach for the right foods if you listen to it. Reconnect and empower your body to support you as a nourished, brilliant woman, shining and luminous!

Hidden Nutrition

In the school of empowerment I share here on my farm, we study two other types of nutrition that are even more important than food. The first is oxygen—you need to get enough or your body processes won't function well. Digestion, elimination, breathing, and carrying nutrition and fresh oxygen to your cells are all very important. That is why working out is claimed to be so healthful. 80% of our detoxification is done through our lungs!

In other words, most of our elimination of wastes is done through breathing. Now we see why yogis do breathing practices! It is a way to detox and heal the body, allowing it to operate better. It's very simple to be aware of the power to breathe and exhale deeply. If we are not getting enough oxygen in our bodies each day, we will reach for more food.

Second are the *high impressions*, which nourish us by filling us with the subtler vibrations of enjoyment, inspiring activities, prayer, uplifting sounds, and nature. We are bombarded by impressions constantly. Are you choosing to focus on impressions that build your spirit, mind, and body?

We practice noticing these impressions and creating healthier ways of processing them. What inspires us in our hearts to get moving through the day? What reminds us of our greatness, our wonder and creativity in the world? How do we fuel our spirits to move forward with our tasks knowing that we are creators and nurturers in life? When we are not receiving higher impressions, we naturally reach for food to fill us.

Paying attention to all three types of nourishment gives you a solid way to approach the art of feeding yourself. Often the reason it is hard to shift our eating patterns is that we are not taking in adequate nourishment from oxygen and high impressions. This makes it harder to change unhealthy eating habits; we must consider these other sources of nutrition.

Take stock of your high impressions first. What are you fueling yourself with? What is nurturing your spirit and can it be improved? How about oxygen—do you always breathe shallowly? Do you get any exercise? Is there any way you can take in more oxygen daily?

Belly breathing alone will provide incredible vitality. I offer a breathing practice in Part Two of the book for you to investigate the beneficial effects of oxygen. These ideas and practices will help to deter emotion-based eating when you are out of sync by getting these three sources of nutrition in balance. Looking at feeding all parts of ourselves and our families as a creative activity, a form of art, a delicious expression of ourselves is a very important step to wellness.

So consider the high impressions, oxygen and then food as your self-nourishing triad. All provide nutrition for your body and work together to run your biological, spiritual machine. Consider all three as you nourish your family. Submerge yourself in the delicious art of feeding yourself and your family. This should be pleasurable, ignite your heart, involve your care, and inspire your sense of taste and beauty. These simple shifts will bring you such health!

Chapter Three
Your Sacred Space

My next shift toward wellness came in 1994 when I started a part-time cleaning business to make extra money. I cleaned two houses twice a week and had a few other girls working for me. I used bleach and the standard cleaners and brands we all know. After just a few weeks I started to feel it in my lungs—these were potent killers I was inhaling.

My hands, even with gloves, were getting red and chafed from the products I used. It was not healthy for me. My body's strong reaction to these products, especially severe during my five hours of work, was a wake-up call. We think that just because things are on store shelves they must be safe. We trust manufacturers and regulations to protect us. I do not leave my health in their hands anymore.

We have been trained to think the smell of bleach or other potent chemical smells mean something is "clean", but they are toxic. Some of us love the smell of toxicity. Consider using lemon or pine, which are nature's cleaners. They smell clean and many chemical cleaners have these scents in them. I got used to the herb-scented, non-toxic cleaners easily. They smell milder and they don't poison you!

You were trained to trust that toxic smell of "clean". Will you keep trusting it in spite of new information about how it harms your health? Try a non-toxic cleaner and learn the healthy smell of clean. Just knowing your products are safer; you don't gag or feel the need to open a window. Switching to natural cleaners, I felt like a better mom and householder. Now when I go in someone's house and they use those common chemical products, I think "toxic", not "clean".

My friend Beth became a member of an environmental company, Melaleuca, which offers environmentally friendly cleaning choices. I signed up and began using their safer products. Learning about what was in our products became my primary mission. It made me realize how much those products affect our physicality. They just aren't healthy. You know it the minute you go near the cleaning aisle and smell the outgassing of that potent mix of toxins.

One thing I learned is that personal care products are unregulated. Hospitals, restaurants, and other businesses have regulatory standards; our homes do not. Your home environment must be regulated by you. The products you choose have a direct impact on your household.

Our bodies absorb things through the skin, our largest organ. Creams, soaps, shampoos, makeup, and clothes all touch the skin directly. Our hands touch counters, dishes, silverware, and the cups we drink from. If all these have chemical residues and small concentrations of toxic ingredients, the toxins build up in our bodies and affect our health. Many believe that allergies and oversensitivity were created by the recent overuse of toxic chemicals in our homes. You may recall the surge in popularity of antibacterial products that quickly faded when we realized they were crippling our immune systems.

Science adapts its way through experimentation. In the science of home care products, we are part of the experiment. We try to kill unwanted organisms and end up killing our own cells and systems. When I was young, products were not as toxic. People used vinegar and baking soda to clean. We are the first generation to live in this toxically "clean" environment.

I saw logic in choosing healthier home products. Over time, I converted to healthier options for everything from lotions to laundry detergents. It was simple to order safe products from Melaleuca. I still use other products but the majority of my home goods are designed not to harm the environment. Our health has been positively affected since I made this choice in 1998. My daughter has rarely needed to go to the doctor and I feel that the non-toxicity of the products I used helped protect her health.

Imagine the Effects

If there is formaldehyde in the products you use, what does that mean for your health? Maybe you believe that it's harmless in small concentrations. But using it to clean and moisturize our bodies, clean and prepare our hair, and put on makeup? Then there are the residues on your dishes, counters, furniture tops, food products, and clothes. There are just too many harmful chemical mixtures around our bodies!

Even in small quantities, toxins affect our health and well-being. We only have one liver to remove all these toxins. We also carry lots of bacteria and other organisms that actually help our systems function properly and toxins are no good for them either! This information made me realize that a healthier home creates a healthier body. Our homes are truly extensions of our bodies!

Living on a farm with a well as our water source made me think about the products people use outside their homes. People put all kinds of chemicals on their lawns just to make the grass green. If they have a well, they might be poisoning themselves. Some people say that the well is too deep to be affected, but our whole water table is connected within the Earth.

The Earth can filter toxins but not in the volume we put out. It's nice to have green, weedless grass, but is it worth sacrificing your health? What happens when you drink water that contains chemical fertilizers and herbicides? Don't be fooled into thinking that it won't affect you.

This book is about vitality. The effects of these small choices add up! Your health and vital energy is affected by the products you use and store in your home environment!! Each small choice comes down to honoring (or not honoring) your body. When you add all of the choices up day after day, year after year, how could they not be part your current state of health?

I have been ordering a portion of my groceries from Melaleuca monthly for over 17 years. It is so much easier to get products delivered than to lug them home! I still perimeter-shop the grocery store and now there are many more opportunities to purchase safer products. It is important that you do. Start with the changes that make sense and are comfortable for you.

Think about skin, body, and hair care. I would rather have fresh plant products like rose and chamomile creams on my face than factory-made chemicals. Good quality skin care products are made with plants because nature is the best healer. All medicines come from her gifts. You should enjoy shampoos and lotions with the real richness of nature. Using organic products smells and feels so luxurious and healthful! Switch what you can and notice all the things that you put on your body from the time you get in the shower until you walk out the door. Buying products with your health in mind goes a long way toward improving your well-being!

Again, try choosing with emotion, making a conscious choice to care about what you have in your home, making certain that it will provide the best place for you and your family to grow. Select the best things with awareness, love and pride. It is creative. It is the art of providing a wonderful sacred space to live.

Your Home Environment

I could write a whole chapter on the next layer of things in your home like paint, carpets loaded with toxins, nonstick cooking pans, mold, electromagnetic energy fields from electronic devices... but I think you have read enough! Just begin with the things that come into contact with your body and you will reap the benefits of making good small choices. Pay attention to the other issues to educate yourself and grow gracefully in this journey.

Build wellness into your plan through awareness. These small choices begin with honoring yourself. You deserve to have the best and safest products for yourself and your home! You can make many beneficial changes with little money. The shift that occurs inside you when you realize that this is important will connect you to a deeper part of yourself.

Your home is your sanctuary from the world. Does it nourish and nurture you to the depths of your being? Creating a nurturing home is the art of our feminine nature. Making good choices for your home settles you, giving you energy, pride and well-being! I encourage you to do what you can to minimize or eliminate the toxicity around you. So many children are affected by allergies or have other sensitivities. Where did this come from? The toxic mix of all our unhealthy products!

Begin to realize that your being doesn't end at your skin, the boundary of your physical body. Our homes, cars and yards are part of the space we live in. Our bodies are capable of great miracles but let's not push their limits by making poor, uninformed choices. There is plenty of science-based information out there about the dangers of the chemicals used in home products. Your health is profoundly affected by what you bring into your home.

The Emotional Effects of Your Sacred Space

Your sacred home should be your safe haven. When you go through your home are you inspired by the color, the furniture, the order, and the beauty? It is so important for women to be in a space that gives us comfort, safety and inspiration. We need to live in a space that motivates and relaxes us so we can be joyful before we go out in the world. Does your family take over your whole house? Are you delighted at the creativity around you in art, books, decorations, layout? With intention, we can make any space nourish us if we understand the necessity of it.

Householder: Holder of the sacred space of the home. Have you noticed that you hold the energy of your home? When you are out of sync, everyone in the house is. This is a very important role, a feminine role. Feng shui is a whole science of organizing your home, reflecting and enhancing your inner and outer life.

At the Vibrant Living Festival we hosted here at Harmony Hill Gardens in 2009, I sat in on a lecture about creativity. The gist of it was how everything around you either gives you energy or drains your energy. To be creative you need to be nourished by things around you. Walk through your house, look around and notice what makes you feel light and joyful, and what makes you feel low, like disorganized areas. Remove things that don't bring you a higher vibration.

Being surrounded by joyful things is what makes you feel nourished, creative and safe. Could you do more to make your home inspire you? You set the tone so the home should be geared to supporting your strong state of being and it will naturally nourish all the others in your home. Feminine essence is nurtured by scents, artwork, flowers, colors, luxurious fabrics, beautiful objects, nature, intriguing literature, plants and cleanliness. A flow, so to speak. Creative, adaptable, flexible, and beautiful.

Find ways to have your home reflect the peace and beauty that you enjoy, that inspires you! Honor your individual way to make a sacred space for all who enter. Show the parts and pieces of life that represent joy, happiness and provide you good energy. This is a wonderful way to cultivate energy for all of life's tasks.

Clear out what is not working! Send any "to do later" dumping grounds (like magazine piles that drain you because you don't have time to read them) out to be reused and recycled. When you see something that takes away your energy, find a way to make it better or clear it up. Otherwise these things will drain your life force on an unconscious level.

Considering the impact of all the choices you make for your home, from cleaning products to decorative items, consciously create your sacred space to support your best expression. Begin with yourself, with what inspires and feels good to you. It will naturally inspire others when you offer your natural, individual way to the world. Nourish your body and your space as an artist and creator in the world!

Chapter Four
Gems of Wisdom

"*Look for [the harmony] and listen to it first in your own heart. At first you may say it is not there; when I search I find only discord. Look deeper. If again you are disappointed, pause and look deeper again. There is a natural melody, an obscure fount in every human heart. It may be hidden over and utterly concealed and silenced—but it is there.... [U]nderneath all life is the strong current that cannot be checked; the great waters are there in reality. Find them and you will perceive that none, not the most wretched of creatures, but is a part of it.... [K]now that it is certainly within yourself. Look for it there, and once having heard it, you will more readily recognize it around you.*"
~ Mabel Collins, 1888 (reprinted in The Theosophical Movement Magazine)

The ability to connect, communicate, and collaborate with others is a feminine quality. We are nourished and energized by doing this. The more we do it, and the wider our circle of care and influence becomes, the healthier we are. Being connected, involved, and surrounded by others creates the circle of life. It nourishes your well-being as well as your family's. Isolation is the start of illness.

I was raised Catholic. I partake in Christianity in that I believe there is a Christos, a sacred consciousness of good of which we are all part. I also believe that whatever religion you are, whatever group or entity you identify with, you are on the correct path if you think about the greatness of existence and make an effort to do good. I honor people by respecting their individual journeys to higher consciousness.

I do not subscribe to the idea that there is only one way to believe and study the great creation we are all part of. We cannot understand it by thinking alone—it is so far beyond our thinking mind. I have a belief system that I use, as we all do. Hopefully it is grounded in real experience rather than just a cultural story. I have chosen to honor all cultural belief systems as philosophies of humanity and it intrigues me to be open to considering the ways of others. Here is the path I followed that allowed me to be open to thinking in religious, scientific, and other ways different than my own.

I was in my early 30s and I babysat small kids to supplement cash flow. Stay-at-home moms get involved in all kinds of ways to bring in money. I worked at the house of a woman named Linda, watching her grandson and my daughter together. She was a wonderful, wise spirit and she had great old books in her house on esoteric philosophies.

My curiosity as a book lover drew me to the shelves to see what was there. Books reveal a lot about people, their interests and their studies. She had a ton of old books on one shelf. They were rich-looking and made you want to touch them—they seemed sacred, old and important. I began reading them during the kids' nap time. One series called *The Word* was like an encyclopedia set filled with great philosophical articles from all religions and ways of life. These books taught me so much rich history through the diverse writings of ancient thinkers on math, religion, astrology science, and language.

Reading about Latin revealed its value as the source of so many of our word roots. Learning their original meanings shed new light on the Latin-based words we use today. So often we overuse the same words (or use too many words) when a greater variety of words would serve us better, and would even give rise to a wider range of feelings for us to experience. Anthony Robbins speaks of using the language better to experience a wider array of feelings.

Linda's books offered a rich study of so many systems that make up our modern education. These books were written in the tradition of Theosophy, which comes from the Greek words *theo* (divine) and *sophia* (wisdom). The only tenet in Theosophy is universal brotherhood. No

Lyn Hicks

cult or sect, just a divine wisdom that includes everyone. You can be any religion and still be a Theosophist.

The plan of Theosophy was to review all philosophies and religions in an effort to see what they all shared. Instead of looking at the differences among them, the tangents and details, it was about finding their similarities in order to reveal the great truth. It didn't make judgments on any of the belief systems, it just sought commonality.

This is where I began to learn more of the similarities between the Eastern traditions and studies and those of my Christian upbringing. Finding common points makes it easier to understand and enjoy other belief systems, not in terms of right or wrong but more as a history of humanity's philosophical thinking and commonality.

This opened my mind to honoring other belief systems. I am not one to say there is a single right way for everyone. We all are unique; we learn things differently and find our paths in life differently. The Dalai Lama would say there are many of the same illnesses but they all have different causes so there are many different cures.

After reviewing different systems from this perspective it became apparent that we are all seeking the same thing—a connection to our greatness, an increased awareness of our brilliance and our mission as we are here to do something good. The golden rule is in all of the belief systems. Some symbol of light is in all of them, as are the ideas of brotherhood and of reaping what you sow.

I feel good knowing I can relate to most people's beliefs and honor their paths and their spiritual journeys rather than selling my own. We need more understanding in this area, especially in this globally interconnected society! Why waste time arguing who has the right story? I'd rather appreciate others where we do have something in common.

As a theosophist you must use discernment. You accept a new belief or way of thinking only if it is supported by your own experience and learning. Nothing is to be taken at face value, even if a great leader or guru told it to you. You are to investigate and sharpen your thinking capacity and determine with your gift of consciousness what awakens and empowers you. It is *your* responsibility.

Like Christian and Native American belief systems, the Eastern traditions—Taoism, Buddhism and Hinduism—all use growing analogies in their writings. As a gardener and grower, this symbolism was easy for me to relate to, so I opened up to these philosophies of ancient times. Many traditions compare our souls to seeds, noting how the appearance of a seed gives no hint of the beauty of the flower that is to come. And that keeping areas clear of weeds helps your flower grow tall and healthy. Clearing your mind is like the process of weeding, removing the life-stealing thoughts so your beautiful thinking can flourish. The caterpillar-to-butterfly analogies also inspired me.

I was able to study it all and honor the writings for my own growth; it created no conflict within my belief system. Opening the door to Eastern thinking is a step toward wellness. We must look at all ways to be whole, not just what we have been taught through our own cultures. There is so much out there in the world that can enhance our lives and release us from our learned limitations!

We are here to experience life, not judge it or make confining rules about how to live it. It is about opening, expanding, appreciating it all. We do way too much thinking and not enough being. Studying Eastern ways creates an awareness in you that opens your mind to the practice of being. Stay open to whatever draws you to understand that. Oprah promoted Eckart Tolle and his ideas about being in the moment, the art of relaxing, being present and noticing what is around you.

I practice yoga and took my first yoga class from a wonderful yogi named Judy, a woman who studied yoga and honored her Jewish culture all her life. Judy was teaching the principles, not just the asanas or poses. I found that yoga thinking expanded my understanding of myself as a spirit filling a body. She called our bodies "vehicles". She taught us that we each have an emotional body, a mental body, and a physical body that our spirits inhabit.

If you haven't ever taken yoga, it is time to investigate and learn about this slow, relaxing way of movement! It is an ancient and rewarding study that helps keep the body flowing and strong on the physical level. Yoga teaches you to stand back and observe your mental chatter, to see that your mind is just one part of your self.

Learning yoga, meditation, and breathing exercises did so much for my health. These practices can teach you new ways to pray if you like doing that, to be present with yourself and the greatness within. This can only be done by settling, by stopping to observe, by stepping out of the chaos we call life. We scurry around so much and these traditions help us understand what it means to relax and calm down.

When the Dalai Lama was driven out of Tibet it came to be considered a gift because now all kinds of ancient traditions can expand beyond national boundaries. We are one humanity so whatever causes one person to seek the great good is the same spark that we all have. Sharing our traditions and blending practices that create peace, calm and openness in our lives is rewarding. We may study and follow a particular belief system but being open and compassionate to other systems will only expand us. We are truly all on one team, a global family. The Eastern concept of the One, the connection between all of us, is important for us to remember. I have benefited by taking tips from these traditions that I can fit with my ideas of what this life experience is all about.

I encourage you to investigate yoga, tai chi, qigong, whichever of these studies comes to you. They offer ways to manage your energy and provide healthful, youth-generating vitality. They have been with humanity for thousands of years, ways to move your body that have been proven by centuries of practice to add health. They teach flexibility and relaxation, helping you notice tightness and move energy through your body gently. Just look around at the influx of this in our country. Yoga and dancing are the most vital movements for women's bodies; they connect us to our flexible and flowing nature.

Being a grower, I can relate to American Indian cultures and beliefs as well. I often feel like a Native American when I am in the garden. Gardening and farming give you a great appreciation for the elements and why American Indians honored their powers. The wind wisps in to dry out winter in March, the rain pours down and feeds the Earth when it needs it most. When the fruits of harvest come forth in fall, we can see why our Thanksgiving celebration was begun.

I can also relate to their use of the Moon as the keeper of time. They had no clocks or calendars so the phases of the Moon were how they described time—"five moons ago", "last full moon", etc. The Moon also governs the tides and the water table. Women's cycles last the same number of days as the Moon phases. In older traditions the Moon represented the feminine essence. People plant by the Moon cycles because the water table is highest at new moon and full moon, so there is a better chance that your seedlings can tap into it. The American Indian traditions have such a magic to them in the ways they work with the Earth and use plants for healing.

Visiting the Southwestern states will spark your connection to American Indians and Earth thinking as well. One July we road-tripped across the country for three weeks with our friends Jake and Terree and our children. We saw so many Indian ruins and spectacular canyons, we couldn't help but feel connected to them, their kivas, their spiritual huts, and their way of peace.

People think they were primitive but they had a respect for life that we need to recover. The wellness of one is the wellness of the whole. You also feel so much smaller among the vast canyons and rock structures. You sense that the world is larger than you know and that greatness is always happening within the universe.

The Vibrant Living Festival I hosted in August 2010 featured many alternative-healing modalities from the ancient traditions. They are all choices in green living, connecting to the Earth and its oils, essences, teas and tinctures. These old ways and traditions offer wisdom and understanding about ourselves and the nature all around us.

The festival ended with a drum circle. I had never experienced one and was mesmerized. This heightened my understanding of how the American Indians used music for healing. We all use music this way. Maybe not consciously but we do. Tone and sound have a huge effect on us. Healing is what drumming and dancing are all about.

The word "shaman" used to scare me. It conjured thoughts of superstition and lower worlds. Learning about Shamanism has been quite an awakening! It is an old form of teaching here on Earth that uses plants, flowers and the parts of nature, sound and the elements to heal and connect us to our essence.

We are made of nature. The lower worlds and dark spirits relate to the past. Some of my past could certainly be characterized as dark spirits or lower worlds! Shamanism offers a beautiful look at life and I consider all alternative medicine as a form of modern Shamanism. It is an expanded worldview that will awaken a flexibility and connectedness in you that is not common here in the West.

Your philosophy, your ideas, and your connections to others are all part of your well-being. The more open you are, the more you nourish your feminine spirit. Being open, being a student of life, investigating and finding ways to connect to others on deeper, more meaningful levels is part of wellness. These are feminine ways. We can find solutions and resolve conflicts among groups that think differently; it is one of our gifts. It is no longer about one group or one way of thinking. That kind of focus separates us from others and limits our experience. It is not about adopting a different belief system. It is about opening up to the vast world of colorful human culture.

We all live and believe in different ways that we learn from our different cultures. It pays to celebrate these differences with honor instead of judgment, to find commonalities and deeper connections with others of different belief systems. This moves you from your head to your whole being, knowing that we are all part of the same humanity. Our diversity makes the world more magical. These are gems of wisdom for all to wear!

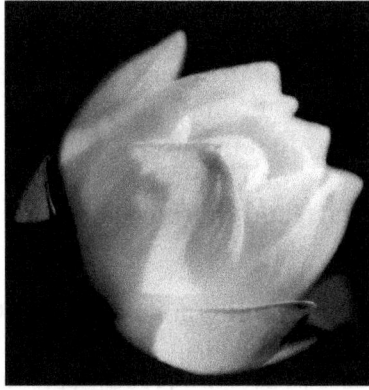

Chapter Five
Artistic Environmentalism

On the farm, artistic environmentalism is a way of life. It is an economic strategy. There never seems to be enough money, so we continually create what we need out of existing things around the farm—old pallets are used to build a compost bin, fences left behind become new barriers for different areas, tires turn into planters. When I hosted a garden camp for children, I would just go into the barn to find things to create with. We painted on slates, used old window frames for projects, made stones and shells into stepping stones, drew on scrap paper, made chimes out of coffee lids, and planted seedlings in yogurt containers. Choosing materials from stuff we already had was part of the fun.

Creating something new out of something old is artistic environmentalism. The whole shabby chic style of interior decorating is just a mix of old furniture and adornments added together, painted, and then resold as a hip new piece. Old metal outdoor furniture adds a sense of eclectic flair—my gorgeous metal gazebo that reminds me of Cinderella's coach came from a farm in New England. It is fun to have something with a history added to your space.

The "recycle and reuse" concept inspires creativity and builds community. We naturally reuse hand-me-down clothes for our kids, and girls like to share from their closets. Parents let children take their used furniture to their first apartment or college dorm. My girlfriends used to have clothing swap evenings where everyone brought some clothes that were just not working for them. We would gather, nourish, share, and go home with some new wardrobe pieces.

The Salvation Army, Purple Heart, and other donation boxes are great places to pass used items along to others in need instead of sending them to landfills. This is such a great community service because we all have so many gently used things that our less fortunate neighbors could reuse. As a parent, when you have small children, this is just the way it is. Extra Pack 'n Plays, bouncy seats, and clip-on chairs get passed from family to family.

Composting leftover food is another great way to reuse and recycle what we have. Composting takes leftovers and turns them into rich soil and nourishment. The process of breaking food waste down into an excellent fertilizer for your plants is rewarding. It is the cycle of life to decompose and go back to the base elements only to be used again for rebuilding.

If you have the space and the interest, composting is a great way to cut down on trash. It cuts your trash volume by more than half. I was amazed how much less garbage I created by making this one living choice. Turning over the compost is almost a meditation—and it's quite a workout. It is a constant reminder that things get used, processed, digested, eliminated, broken down, and reused. It is just the cycle of life. The critters that break down the food are vital to the process. All things have their place, even the dark, creepy ones!

Our experiences and emotions also go through this cycle; we are truly just following a rhythm, a pattern. I know composting is not for everyone. It offers a great lesson in the circle of life and gives you a deeper appreciation for the less beautiful things. Even our horrible experiences can be turned into great learning that nourishes us.

When you recycle, it's amazing how much you can actually cut down on waste. I was so glad when we started to recycle the paper monster that was in our home. Packaging, boxes and food containers travel a long way just to be discarded. Recycled paper does save trees. Truly one of the best things you can do for the Earth is plant a tree! They offer shade, reduce your air conditioning bills if planted near your home, filter your air, provide homes for animals, create cool spots, and of course add beauty!

Try to be more conscious about purchasing recycled paper—demand creates the market. Recycling product packaging and food containers cuts down on garbage as well. They say a third of our landfill volume is taken up by packaging materials. When you get some product that seems to have more container than contents, you can see why. These practices are changing; we are using more renewable resources for packaging and shipping. The waste in our current system is unnecessary and gluttonous.

We can donate our old cell phones for reuse by people in crisis. They are collected all over. The Lions Club collects old eyeglasses for redistribution to those who need them. There are so many junk collectors who make a killing on things they gather from others. There is a market for recycling scrap metal so people will come get your old washer or stove. Books can be reused many times and recycled. Philadelphia held a big computer-recycling day where they rebuilt old computers for those who couldn't afford them. Technology gets old so fast—I am thankful someone can rebuild computers, allowing others to access the Internet so they can connect with the world.

I always reuse vases for my weekly flower customers. Many people drop off their vases at our farm when they are clearing their cabinets in spring and fall. I reuse them and save some money on events or save them for when I donate flowers. It is truly interesting the creative ways we can find to keep things out of the dump. It makes for a more rhythmic way of using our resources, consciously engaging more of ourselves in the simple tasks of life.

Vintage stores are really hip these days. You can get great prices on all kinds of items and so many people report such finds in them. My sister had a '70s party and the vintage store offered us some fashion to wear. Used clothing stores keep those old prom dresses and formal clothes in circulation, not hidden in your closet. And they help keep the local economy flowing!

Fabrics and materials of all sorts can be re-purposed. The interior design and fashion fields are starting to focus on reducing waste. Using fewer resources will help reduce product prices. The old "trash to treasure" adage is alive and well. It makes sense and we need to consider our children when we buy new things or clean out the house. Consumerism is unnecessarily wasteful done in the way of our current system.

I think the creativity of the green movement is astounding! I love all the fashion and building practices that have cropped up from this "re-purposeful" thinking. Those purses Terracycle makes from candy wrappers are just over-the-top creativity. This is the way things will be made in the future. Extending the cycle of life of our resources just seems so smart.

I call this "artistic environmentalism" and it goes back to the principles of our forefathers. They had little and made do with what was about. It is creative, fun and exciting to watch what emerges out of life's leftovers—like when you make some incredible dinner out of that odd mix in your refrigerator.

You don't have to be worried about your finances to institute this green practice. The feeling you get from helping someone by sharing goes a long way towards improving your well-being and saves our resources to boot. It offers us the opportunity to look for creative answers, to add artistry to our lives and engage more than just our minds. Clearing things out is a deeper experience when you know your efforts will help someone else. It connects you more deeply to the cycle of life.

Challenge yourself to be more aware of how you can help the larger community as you use things each day. How might others benefit from your old things? How can you add to the cycle of resources so we have some left for future generations? This doesn't have to be difficult or time-consuming. A small change in your connection to the larger world will naturally allow you to be more conscious of your part in things. Knowing you are in a web of life and that you choose to honor your place and share with those who are coming next, helping where you can. You will feel better because of these choices, knowing you are part of an important shift in the larger community toward a greater awareness of resource consumption. Sharing and caring—it's an art in living that comes naturally to women!

For Lyn's Take on Using Femininity in All Your Life, visit www.LotusProjectBook.com

Chapter Six
Garden Goddess Wisdom

Throughout our lives we enjoy feeling the power of nature. We vacation in the great outdoors for a good reason. It heals and relaxes us on so many levels—subtle levels whose existence we don't yet remember. It nourishes our hearts, our breath, our lungs, our power to take in life. These impressions remind us of joy, an important factor in our well-being. To truly understand how much this connection means to us on many levels, you must come to understand it so you can draw on nature's energy for yourself. It begins with connecting with nature and just knowing how good it makes you feel.

Our planet is called "Mother Earth" and the force of it "Mother Nature" because she reflects the creative principle. She is the place where life grows. When you stop to notice nature, you relax. You get back into the moment that is the creative place. Your mind stops chattering, you notice the birds, the clouds, the light… Something shifts and you receive high impressions. A subtle lightness and openness arises. This shift is healing; it is the power of nature. You don't have to do anything; you will fill up if you are conscious of the process. Just being in nature, you find simple, present joy.

What I am saying is *get out in nature*! It balances you. It feeds your body, mind and heart. It heals you. Why? Because it nourishes you. You become the energy receiver, receiving beauty, calmness, space, openness, wonder. Scientifically, it is about ions. Nature provides negative ions that balance you. (More on this shortly.)

Whatever state you are in, you will naturally relax if you tune into nature. This is an oxytocin space, so easy to receive. You just fill up and balance. Think about it. Where do you vacation? Why do you vacation there? When you think about this you see yourself relaxing with nothing to do but take in the scenery and enjoy. Relax and absorb what is around you now. You can do this daily, anytime. Take a minute to notice nature and her healing.

My Nature Story

The story of Harmony Hill Gardens begins with the farm I landed on to bring up my only daughter—such a wonderful place to raise yourself and a child! Surrounded by beauty, fresh air, old wise trees, a babbling creek, a pond and lots of open land to create on. Rooted in Bucks County, Pennsylvania, an affluent spot with gorgeous homes, wonderful respites, culture and flair. The farm was not so picturesque when I first arrived. It wasn't one of the beautiful ones all done to the nines. It was more run down, overgrown and unkempt, yet it offered us an opportunity to uncover its wonder. The nature around it called me.

I grew up with a garden. In fact, my dad's parents had a farm. All my grandparents were Polish immigrants transplanted from New York City to the coal mining regions of Pennsylvania. They grew most of their food for themselves, canning, making jellies and sustaining themselves from the land. One side lived in the town, grew and raised food in the yard; the other was in the outskirts with acres to farm.

My dad always had a garden full of cucumbers, tomatoes, and peppers. He grew sooo many tomatoes! We always ate tomatoes with salt and pepper, sliced cucumbers in vinegar and salt, and peppers in a bowl with every meal in summer. The remnants of the victory gardens so necessary during the war inspired my dad to have a plot in our yard. I enjoyed eating the fresh grown vegetables; it was just the way it was.

When I moved to Harmony Hill Gardens the first thing I did was make a vegetable garden. The art of planting, growing, harvesting and cooking your own food is empowering. You completely understand the term "Mother Earth". Mother Maya, a teacher of Ayurvedic medicine, has a whole book on the power of healing with food. The growing, the harvesting, and the cooking are her cures for most ills. Reconnecting with the creative spirit of the Earth, plants, and nourishment honors this process, the feminine art that is grounded in our gatherer roots. Mother Maya offers a view of nourishing ourselves that heals our feminine spirit.

Lyn Hicks

She is a favorite guide for me as a woman.

I so enjoyed gardening as many people do. There is something meditative about it. You get lost in nature as you tend it, not sure what you are thinking about or if you are just doing and there is no thinking at all. We love being in nature with the smell and feel of the soil. We are closely connected to the Earth but we are not taught that.

You are okay when you garden. It is hard work and at times painful and tedious to toil with weeds, yet it clears your head like cleaning your house sometimes can. You feel accomplished, peaceful and nourished when you are done. I enjoyed my garden so much that I thought it was the next financial gift that would unfold.

However, after the amount of time it took to pick a bunch of cherry tomatoes (there are many, many per plant), I would have wanted to charge $10 per pint! I knew then that I wouldn't make money gardening. Vegetable plants yield a ton of produce. You must harvest each plant daily or vegetables like beans get too big with huge seeds. I liked to pick what I needed just when I wanted to cook it. The bounty was so great on a few plants that my sporadic picking was going to inhibit their ability to offer fruit. The idea of growing vegetables for a living lost its luster.

Gardening inspired me. I loved to play in the dirt and engage the Earth like I did when I was young. My childhood friend Sheila and I would go to Neshaminy Creek and pretend we had no family and had to survive. We created so many great adventures in our minds while we explored outside—a connection so many kids are missing these days.

Growing was a contrast to the professional jobs I have had throughout life—more playful, more free. I began growing flowers and an *aha!* moment hit. Harvesting flowers is one of the most lovely things in the world. We all love flowers! Watching them open then bloom, picking them for friends and for your home, there is nothing more lovely than that. Flowers are also the highest-paying crop and I knew I could earn some money growing them. Plus I would get the joy of working in the garden and the fun of arranging the flowers for others.

Spending my days meandering through the flowers was the beginning of Harmony Hill Gardens. From there the gardens just grew and grew. We kept having to create more plots so I could grow some of those and those and those.... It is almost like a sickness for growers; you must try everything and buy way more plants and seeds than you have room for.

I decided to try organic growing because it seemed easier than trying to learn all the other ways that growers use to manipulate conditions. I didn't really want to learn about all the science and chemicals—I didn't want to be responsible for mixing them up. I'd had enough of chemicals after the cleaning experience anyway, so I began just using compost and fish emulsion. I still use only these!

I inter-planted and spread my crops into multiple areas. That is how I manage bugs, diseases and whatever else comes up. Sometimes the crop just doesn't make it because of beetles, water needs, or bad seed. Every year brings unpredictable conditions and if you are going to field grow in nature, that is just how it is. There may be a failure one year but there is always something else that unexpectedly goes gangbusters so it balances out.

I did consider using chemicals to control situations, as many growers do. In the second season I had trouble with thrips on my gladiolas so I spoke to my supplier and he only offered me conventional chemical treatment. I bought it and was taking it out to spread on the bed when I just stopped dead in my tracks. I waited a moment and just couldn't do it. It didn't seem right so I never spread the chemicals.

It was a defining moment. I can't explain it, it wasn't a mental decision, I just did not pour out the poison. Instead I took it to the tech school's yearly hazardous waste pickup for safe disposal. Don't ever dump out your poisons. Check your local government website for hazardous and electronic waste drop-off dates!

Nature Lessons

The lessons you learn by working with plants are so profound they are spiritual. You start to understand the ancient traditions more clearly because their wisdom is based on growing analogies. So you do the process while you consider the mental aspect—experiential learning. Small, plain-looking seeds turn into incredibly tall plants that produce big, beautiful blooms. You remember the magic beans in the tale of Jack and the Beanstalk. Often the smallest seeds produce the biggest flowers. Lots of old sayings begin to make sense, like "bloom where you are planted" and "the seed foretells nothing of the beauty that will come".

My honor for nature flourished as I realized the power of growing things. The seeds are so powerful they can grow with or without you. You also find the meaning of *being* as opposed to *doing*. You can sit in the garden

Lyn Hicks

some days with no thoughts at all, just absorbing and experiencing the sensory perception that abounds all about.

This is how I learned of the great energy nature provides. I could feel it just bubbling up inside me—relaxed, safe, carefree, open. You reach incredibly high states of joy just being outside. The colors and the beauty are astounding. You find yourself talking to the plants as though they were your friends, welcoming perennials in the spring, and watching for things to bloom each day. Nature's joy just fills us.

Anyone who has a landscaped yard knows this feeling. Nature does something to calm you, to connect you and still you. We all vacation in naturally beautiful spots surrounded by the forest, the beach, or the mountains. We feel the magic and can't put it into words. It calls us to explore the Earth and preserve our outdoor environment. We are missing this too much of the time, and the green movement is here to remind us!

Nature heals. You can feel and absorb this healing. Consciously notice what happens next time you go out in nature. Does it comfort you? Do you notice that problems just fade away, intensity softens and things seem more settled?

Start to deepen your connection to nature. It is here that you will see the nourishing feminine principle and sense your feminine essence. You may not all be gardeners but you know the connection I am speaking of. It may not be through digging in the soil. It may be sitting with your flower box on the back patio to relax after a long day at work. It may be hiking at the nature center with a friend or being in your backyard on the swing set with a child. It may be hearing the call of that bunch of flowers in the store checkout aisle.

Nature calls you too as her creator, birthing whatever you want in life. She offers a vast energy source that we have yet to harness, creative relaxed energy that is available, easily found, calming. Tune into it when you are tired, depressed, or off balance and see what it offers.

All things, technology included, are composed of atoms. In technology, positive ions (positively charged atoms) are the base and negative ions (negatively charged atoms) are suppressed. The negative ions represent the feminine side of the atom. Remember that if an atom is a negative ion, it will try to reach balance by uniting with positive ions. They share electrons to balance their charges and electron fields, thus creating a molecule.

Much of the technology in our homes creates unbalanced positive ions that seek negative ions, using our bodies or whatever they can find to supply them. We are surrounded by these positive ions inside our homes, while nature is filled with negative ions. That is why it balances us. It responds to those unstable atoms that are seeking the suppressed negative ions.

Scientifically, nature balances the atoms in our body on this basic level. This is one reason we receive such healing from nature. It's also a clue to why so much feminine energy is missing from homes today. Do computers, televisions, air conditioners and other home technologies hurt our bodies? You can wait for the studies but there is already evidence that they do. This drain on our bodies at the atomic level must be balanced out. Nature provides these suppressed parts of the atom to create balance and healing.

Sexual Energy

Sexual, creative energy drives the world of nature. The bees, flowers and all creatures move about in an effort to reproduce. This same sexual energy is used in the creation of all things—a new job, a better marriage, a dream business, even a love for yourself and your being.

Women have been taught to use this magnetism solely to attract men. We can also use it for self-development and allow it to enhance our individuality, our hearts, our voices and creations, our purpose, and the great connection to all. Women have a lot of problems in our reproductive systems that reflect this misunderstanding. It is okay to be alluring, playful, meandering and sensual—not only when we are attracting men, but in all life. Not in a sexual way, in a creative way. Charm, flexibility, passion, collaboration—these are natural, healthy byproducts of sexual energy that we can use to be more inspired and alive!

In the real truth of the tale, women are the flowers of humanity. We flower and produce the seeds necessary for the great human experience to continue. We are the microcosm of the macrocosm. Finding what that means to you deep within is a secret to becoming the gorgeous, unique, exquisite, vital, blooming flower you were meant to be. Somehow women got the "less than" label in society while in nature, there is an equal balance of male and female energy in creation. Humanity at large must reconnect to this real balance. Most importantly, we as women need to claim our power as equal and complementary.

Lyn Hicks

Nature reminds us to receive as well as give. You receive by just sitting with her. Others receive from us by just sitting with us. We do not always have to be moving at high speed, missing the beauty all about. We must reawaken our connection to this creative power in ourselves. So many women say they are not creative. Really? Your biology has the most miraculous creative ability in our world. How can we be so disconnected from our bodies as to think we don't have creativity?

Most of our body is geared toward this power of creation. Sit with that. Realize that there is a power within you. You can acknowledge its brilliance and tap into it. As a woman, you are naturally, biologically geared toward creation. Your hormones, your organs, and your body are designed to create new life.

It is natural and perfect for us to use this system in all areas of life. We are creating the environments, the people, the spaces around us already. Own that power in joy! Own that power as much as you own your ability to be productive, complete tasks, and race around. There is a natural flow to how we move, like the water if we remember it. We are equipped to make the most beautiful world that could exist if we use our power to recreate this space together.

This shift within me was so profound that I have dedicated the next phase of Harmony Hill Gardens to giving birth to The Lotus Project, a sustainable green venue that hosts experiential workshops on creativity and empowerment in the midst of nature. A place to remember the creative energy that nature offers every day, and to chime in with our own. This is who we are in the opposing and complementary forces that create this world. Equal, powerful, creative, receptive, open, nurturing, and needed to beautify our current world.

For Lyn's Take on
Connecting to Nature, visit
www.LotusProjectBook.com

Chapter Seven
Modern-Day Shamanism

Vitality, well-being and happiness. All are states we want to achieve, buzzwords almost because we see so much about them. But what do they really mean? I *looked* healthy and fit. I was using all the organics and eating well, connecting to nature and enjoying the moment.

But I still didn't have a handle on how to move about in the relaxed safe way of oxytocin, so I often still ran about like a headless chicken. One Thanksgiving I landed in the hospital. I thought it was my appendix but it turned out to be a large ovarian cyst. Lovely! Once I recovered a bit, my gynecologist told me it was a grave situation. There was nothing to be done but to get ultrasounds every three months and watch it. In the meanwhile, if the pain got bad enough, he would see me in the emergency room. Comforting.

I walked out in a panic. It seemed like I needed to do something to help my reproductive system, but there were no directions. This is when I became very thankful for alternative medicine and my practitioner, Dr. Lauren Nappen. I knew her in high school, but I didn't know she had an office behind my mother-in-law's just waiting for me to visit!

I went in with my problem and she just giggled as she does. Suddenly, I relaxed and thought, "Oh, maybe I shouldn't be so serious?" Thank goodness for that hopeful moment when I wasn't feeling doomed anymore. What is it about that when we think we are doomed? It's so silly to attach dark gloom to things unnecessarily.

She told me the cyst was either going to shrink naturally or burst and they would take it out. She made it sound so matter-of-fact and not grave at all. We tested muscle to see if nutritional support would help and I got some herbs and whole food supplements. I left feeling like it was no big deal. Lauren just let me know that the sky wasn't falling in so I switched focus, becoming less attached to my illness. I was thankful just to relax about it for a little while.

Alternative healing is just that. An alternative path to conventional methods. It encompasses many modalities and can be used in addition to Western ways! All medicine is good and you use what you need at the time.

Be open to investigating alternative healing. If you have an ailment that you can't seem to manage with Western medicine, if you have no ailment and just need to balance on a different level, or if you are in a transforming phase of life, this is a path you should explore. We are whole beings thus we are holistic, meaning we encompass more than just our bodies and we emanate layers of energy, whether we believe it or not.

Science has shown that we have an electromagnetic field that extends beyond our physical body. We are constantly mixing that field with the energies of others. So "wholeness" encompasses your emotions, your mental state, your nutrition and how you treat all these parts. We must understand that we have more than physical things going on.

My cyst helped me realize I had to connect more deeply with my body and its messages. What energy are we bringing to life? We need to get to where we are bringing good, clean, light energy to share with others. Are you lethargic, filling yourself with food, shopping or other unconscious patterns that you can't seem to shake? Does your body send you messages of tiredness, illness, or pain that you are not listening to? Alternative healing fills the gap left by current medicine, offering many other ways to approach ourselves and our issues.

We are always moving around on our moving planet in our moving universe. We think there will come a time when all is well and we have arrived at balance. It is more like you are in balance for a moment then get off balance again. To grow, you must expand and change. You have to keep moving and changing to get back in balance. Alternative healing addresses you in this way, giving you tools to find where you are in space and redirecting you toward balance. It is continual; change is always happening, conditions are always in flux.

Thus began a great magical part of my journey! Lauren offers so many healing modalities that are all tied to the Earth. She is a chiropractor, does nutrition with Standard Process, and practices homeopathy and Reiki. Her gifts also include reconnective healing and working with flower essences and essential oils. I underwent an evaluation and three months of weekly followup care. It has been perfect for this time in my life. Midlife, married, my only child just left for college and here I am in the world again to be me! Lyn.

Wow! Huge! Not that I was ever someone else but I had such a strong focus on raising a child and made all my choices with her well-being in mind. Not to have to mother anyone but me was a huge change! It sounded good... if I only knew what to do. Receiving help from this nontraditional healing mode helped me tremendously by caring for my ovary as well as other parts of me that were in transition.

What to do? How many times have we been there? As if the whole picture is just going to flash before our eyes in a moment. It doesn't! Spirit comes in the side door for an unexpected surprise visit. It was the perfect moment to tie together some pieces of this bridge time in life.

Aligning, essentials oils and flower essences seemed to match my needs. Flowers have a great presence; they are here to help with our healing. We are made of plant, animal and mineral kingdoms. Of course fresh and tinctured they would have a pleasing effect on my body and soul during my transition time. I worked with them with such amazement—their beauty is just the beginning of their healing! They are foods *and* medicine, ladies.

So my husband and I became empty nesters. A lot of change occurred and continues for us as individuals and as partners. This is a pivotal time and my wisdom tells me that I am a creator. With all my years of experience, this is the most aware I have been in my life that I am capable of consciously designing these next years. A deeper understanding that you *create* your life has come upon me.

As a mother you are so excited to see your child thrive and spread her wings. There is also a sense of loss of that hands-on motherhood, those parenting skills that can rest now that less focus and guidance is needed from you. This leaves a lot of open space for women at these transition times when roles fall away—identities, really. I realized that I too was a bird getting wings. As a mom and role model, I too had to express more parts of my self to the world, to grow further and fill those spaces that are

Lyn.

I should have been more consciously aware of this along the way: I should have taken more time for self-development to make it a habit. As a mom, so many other things crowded my attention. Although sadness was part of this new life situation, I felt it, shed my tears and dove into some new things that unexpectedly appeared on the horizon. I leaped toward things that I observed coming to me in my life. The second part of this book shares my new findings, offering practices to energize your whole being. These are things that I found enjoyable, empowering and transforming.

We can find these things right around us when our lives are shifting. Just notice, increase your awareness and really look. You don't need a big plan, just watch as you open to fill the space. We are always blessed with the next step in our unique paths. Sitting until the fog lifts is not favored in our society. However, slowing down to pay attention to what is all about us is a feminine way. Seeing the whole field without the blinders is important for humanity at this time.

I have dreamed of what I would do with this next phase of life for a while. Fortunately, Lauren told me to just notice all that was about me. This is a very important step toward wellness. Don't look only inside the blinders of what you *think* will happen and what you *think* your transition plan should be. Try to be open to seeing the wide, clear field ahead of you. Wise, wise advice from Lauren. During these larger shifts it pays to go inside and see what is happening. Get out of your mind and feel your heart, your essence, your inner friend who talks nicely to you. I often just put on rose-colored glasses and move ahead with a positive attitude. Put a happy face on it.

This is okay if you do it consciously, not as a response mechanism as so many of us have done for so long. See where you are in all the truth, accept the sad or scary parts, then move toward where you want to go. A bit different than just putting on a happy face. We and the world can no longer pretend that change will come if we keep following the old ways.

Modern medicine is backing up the thinking that is offered in nontraditional medicine. Deepak Chopra, Andrew Weil, Louise Hay and others have created a bridge for us all. Opening us to the knowledge that we are more than just physical symptoms and that our emotions, thoughts and behavior also effect our health.

My first experience with alternative healing was when I was seeking ways to quit smoking. After trying prescription medicines, I went to a hypnotist, acupuncturist, and an intuitive healer. Dawn Marie was the first out-of-the-box experience I had. I was at a business card exchange. I had read about flower essences and decided I needed some lotus essence. So I wrote it down on my to-do list. I attended this card exchange and Dawn Marie stands up and says she is an intuitive healer and makes flower essences. I had a feeling I never had before, like a laser of awareness went to her.

Afterwards I took her card and left her a message to get some essence and have her explain her intuitive healing. I have read some of Carolyn Myss's books on this. When she called back she said she did readings on the phone. I thought it was odd but I still felt I wanted to schedule one. I had recently lost my dad to cancer and my husband had just lost his brother to a heart attack. I needed a reading because grief was everywhere around me. My friends thought I was crazy and wondered how much it would cost. I went for it anyway. Intuitively it seemed right.

What I learned from my reading transformed how I looked at life. Dawn Marie told me that I had denied my clan. I thought that was interesting because I always felt like the black sheep of my family, like I was denied by them. When I considered that I had possibly closed myself off to their love, it shifted my perspective dramatically. I only had that one reading and it opened me up. I felt less victimized and more responsible. My lesson was to connect those in my family who were different than me, a twist on being shunned for not fitting in. This widened perspective made a foundational shift in my life.

It is all just perspective anyway. There are so many ways to see things. Often at transition times that larger look at things is refreshing! I have felt open to people my whole life. I can find a good quality in almost everyone. I am open to new ways of thinking and I stretch myself to learn others' perspectives. This is truly a gift and Dawn Marie's commentary allowed me to see the greatness of that gift and move forward without my old "black sheep" thinking.

A few years later I finally went to see Lauren after thinking of her, reading about her in a few local magazines, then seeing her at a business gathering. I was open to a new way of thinking and wanted to feel in charge of my health. She is so helpful with all her modalities, teaching us that we are greater beings than we appear to be. Her brilliant gift is offering advice on change. She takes the details and drama out of the situation so you can see the core issues, allowing you to make choices more congruent with the being you are becoming.

On the first Monday evening of the month, she hosts a gathering called "Wellth of Soulutions". All are welcome to come to this healing space together. She shares one of her color therapies or oils, we do an exercise with it, she speaks her magical wisdom, we call on the light and place people and situations into it (ourselves too!) and we leave transformed, feeling camaraderie and taking responsibility for our happiness. We are all there trying to find peace and stillness for reflection and calm. It's more powerful when it's done in a group!

Learning to slow down, to be still and just receive has brought me health and wellness. This is sacred femininity!

Are you aligned? Do you know what you are doing and where you want to go? Or are you just rolling from one task to the next, exhausted and in a state of emergency and panic? Living in your adrenal system this way will cause you problems! These are the kinds of problems alternative healing helps solve. There are lots of gifted healers out there. One will show up if you are interested. Take the hint you are sensing and learn how much more you are than just a physical body.

My journey in alternative thinking has been an evolution through years of checking things out. I am a yogi and I practice yoga most days. It gets the fire going, as our yoga teacher Judy would say. I trade flowers for a monthly massage. I so appreciate this trade! Deepak Chopra, Andrew Weil, Christine Northrop and Mother Maya are just a few whose books have opened me up to alternative healing. It is part of the green, feminine nurturing movement because it reminds us to honor ourselves by using gifts from the Earth and to notice our larger connection to things.

There is much transformation in our thinking these days so I do like to investigate things that seem magical. The great mother willow tree has medicine for me? Healing can occur just sitting near her? I like it when the world is more mystical than we were taught. You will see things that way once you open up to the possibilities. There are so many ancient traditions to partake of! We all sing different tunes so find one that seems real to you to investigate.

Follow your gut, your intuition, the sense that comes through your feeling nature. I call this medicine Shamanism because so many of the roots of alternative healing came from the shaman. They were the healers of the community and their ills, using herbs and plant medicines, Reiki energy, and the study of levels of being beyond our consciousness.

It is such a vast universe and expanding our thinking beyond right or wrong, black or white opens up many great ways to remind us we are okay. This green lifestyle choice is so worth making. Your life and world will become magical again!

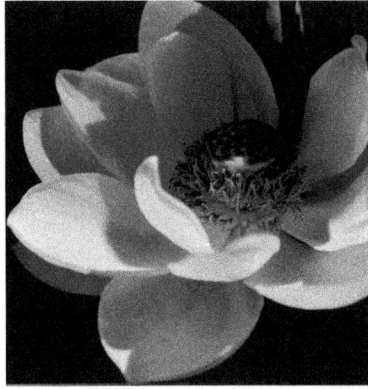

Chapter Eight
Release and Rejuvenate

There is a law of existence that is rarely mentioned—the law of sacrifice. Maybe we don't hear about it because nobody likes the name! It is an important law that is considered to precede the law of attraction. The law of sacrifice states that we must give up something in order to allow something new to enter our lives. We often forget this. Yes, we expand and our influence grows, but a life is like a container. If it is filled to the brim how can new things fit?

In some beliefs they say that right on the perimeter of your world there is a place filled with stuff just waiting to become manifest, waiting for a space to be. This concept reminds us to make space for more health and wholeness by getting rid of old, worn out patterns, ideas, items, and negative memories that are no longer serving us well.

It is not about sacrificing things that you love or that give you great joy. It is about letting go of the unnecessary things you are carrying, the way that trees drop their leaves in the fall. Our minds carry so much baggage that clogs the space for new thinking and new joys. Using the law of sacrifice can take you far in the journey toward greater well-being.

We practice this law during spring and fall cleaning. We go through our stuff and give away old toys and clothes. We clean our cars, our desks, our basements. We go to spas to slough off old skin, cleaning our outer bodies. Yet the bulk of the *garbage* is inside our bodies. It is no secret that our food producers care about profits at least as much as they care about public health. This is slowly changing but we still choose unhealthy options even when better ones are available! So, how best to clean our bodies of unhealthy food and toxins?

My sister wanted to do a purification with Standard Process supplements through our alternative healer, Dr. Lauren. She wanted to lose some weight for her upcoming Dominican adventure. I have tried some fasts; I did the Master Cleanse for one day a week for four weeks in the spring and fall. Many have professed the importance of clearing, fasting, and cleansing to promote greater body health. In 4th Century BC, Hippocrates, considered the "Father of Medicine", recommended periodic fasting to cleanse and rest the digestive track. 16th Century Paracelsus, renowned physician, called fasting the "greatest remedy, physician within." In India yogis and Ayervedic medicine has promoted health through internal cleansing. The Native Indians here used sweatlodges to cleanse internally. Europeans have long enjoyed saunas and bathhouses in many of their cultures. Many religious sects fast certain times of the year. So this is not new health news to utilize this for healing.

I decided to be my sister's support. She was worried she would eat chocolate and not follow the program. I thought it would be easy since I had already given up sugar and wheat. (This was not by choice but because I had discovered allergies to them. My skin would get rashes when I ate those things, and when the rash showed up on my face I got serious about changing my diet.) As it turned out, I cheated on the cleanse more than my sister did!

We went to a lecture presented by Standard Process and learned so much about our bodies and how various additives affect us. We learned that some cookies contain 25 appetite enhancers. (They are listed as artificial flavorings.) Wow! No wonder we eat so many at a sitting. That was enlightening in itself!

The main focus of the presentation was cleansing the liver. This organ is so overworked that it often can't do all of the functions it is designed for. The kidneys and bladder were targeted for cleansing as well. The company has a farm in the Midwest where it grows vegetables organically and then dries them for use in their food supplements. The late founder, Dr. Leeds, started curing people with alternative medicine back in the 1930s.

Why do we not investigate when we hear of these folks? Are we so untrusting that we won't believe in anyone else's ways? Watching news reports about our mainstream medicine system doesn't inspire me to trust either. Alternative medicine is just a different way to look at health. Might as well be curious about alternative viewpoints these days, given our current state of health and health care!

Standard Process offers whole foods to support our systems in an effort to help our bodies balance. Quite a wise concept! Boosting the immune system makes sense! Standard Process has a purification program that involves powdered shakes made with lots of greens, broccoli, and brussels sprouts as well as fruit or vegetables and water. These shakes taste good and they help cleanse your intestine as well.

They also have supplements made of more vegetables to take as you go through the cleanse. The program is to eat 3/4 vegetables and 1/4 fruit for 21 days. They highly recommend using organic produce where possible. At day 11 you can add in lean proteins. You slowly add other foods back in when you are done and notice how they affect you. These effects are surprising and very interesting.

I learned so many ways to cook and eat vegetables during those 21 days. I roasted up, stir-fried, souped and saladed way more vegetables than I even knew existed, and the flavors were really eye-opening! The Standard Process program expanded my repertoire of food immensely. My husband loved the new veggies and the ways I used them as well.

The cleansing program was more of a mind game than anything. Some people only made it a few days. I went the whole way but I wasn't always faithful to it. There were days I thought I would die without bread, so I ate some. One night I ate four ice cream bars. I felt so sick the next morning and was slow the whole day because I hadn't nourished my body properly.

I didn't beat myself up, just kept going like we do in life. The cleanse was an exercise in noticing how foods effect us, not self-rejection. On the low-spirit days I definitely came up against my old eating patterns, trying to feed my emotions as though it would really help. It was a good exercise in seeing how we relate to food and how we use it for much more than energy management. I felt proud in the end and more aware of my unconscious eating habits.

The cleansing program added vitality and variety as it cleared my system. I highly recommend this as a step into well-being. You learn to value organic foods because you see the good effects they have on your body. Whether you choose this cleanse or some other way to clear and rest your digestive system, your body will be grateful. Our basic self runs all our systems and it too needs nourishment and appreciation! That physical level that so brilliantly makes our hearts beat thrives when it is honored and cleaned.

Just noticing when you eat and what you want to eat after a bad day or a fight gets you in touch with what you do to nourish yourself, how you do it and why. Then there is a slew of cultural eating that you overlook—things that remind you of home, comfort, or your Nana. Standard Process truly had a revolutionary impact on me and how I fuel my engine today.

As we get older we change and we need different nutritional support than younger people with growing bodies. It is important to see what makes your unique being soar. They say people change all their cells every seven years, some more often. That offers a lot of room to change and become a healthier human.

I found the purification program to be about so much more than food and my liver. Memories, old illnesses, layers of heavy stuff finally got a chance to move out! It was a sacrifice, a purging, a cleansing. Digestion affects all our levels of being—mental, physical, and emotional. We are truly a digestive fire, taking in new things, digesting them, making them into useful building blocks and releasing the waste. We do this on all our levels of experience. Doing it consciously in unison through a purification program is a great exercise for health. It is like the cycle of the seasons.

In Aharaj yoga, we clear the emotions through energizing movements called *katas*. I have also cleared my emotions through free form writing and journaling. Meditation and being in the moment helps settle the mind. Clearing the body takes time as well. This kind of purification works with the law of sacrifice as we clear out our insides to allow for the growth of new ideas, feelings and doings. The older you get, the more you realize that we are involved in cycles of all kinds. Being green and vital is about riding them, using them, flowing with them. Releasing like the leaves in the fall, or tilling the empty ground in spring gives you two good cycles to ride with some fasting practice.

In Part Two of this book, I offer a practice called conscious eating. It involves paying attention to how we eat, what we take in, and what is around us. The idea of green living is to become more wrapped up in the process or activity you are doing, so your life becomes a yoga practice and all tasks become richer experiences for you.

All the choices you make can inspire you more deeply than they do now. Just doing what you are doing is hard when your mind is always rushing.

Lyn Hicks

Making repetitive tasks more nourishing and conscious grounds you more in being than in thinking. This way your life becomes richer each moment in movement. You become more settled and relaxed, knowing your choices enhance your well-being. Release and rejuvenate, empty and fill. Fill consciously with the finest in life!

Lyn Hicks

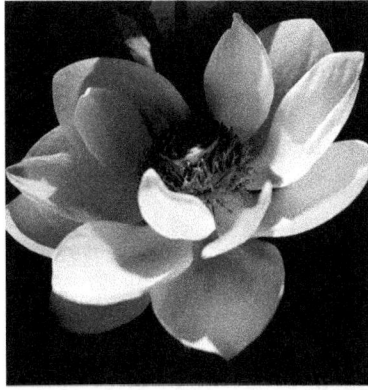

Chapter Nine
Energy Management

Energy management! The green movement will be fueled by our increased ability to use renewable resources to generate energy as demand grows for the Earth's depleted oil supply. Wind power, water power, solar power, electric cars... All of these are expanding so that we can supply and use energy without polluting our world.

The whole green building movement is about energy efficiency. Building homes with tighter envelopes so we don't lose heat and cooling. Using renewable lumber, energy-efficient appliances and local materials that reduce our carbon footprint. Creating what we need in a more responsible way. As the economy shifts toward energy efficiency, whatever way you can support this important movement will help it expand and preserve natural resources.

Looking at this in a different way, how do we use the energy *within* ourselves to do our tasks? This is the energy management I want to talk about. How do we manage our personal energy—the resources inside ourselves and our bodies? With so much to do and not enough time or energy to do it all, it comes down to how you manage your energy and your time in order to get the most out of them.

This is an area where we need to gain control so we can have more relaxed lives. As women, this is very important for us to understand. In the past, women could work at a much slower pace; we didn't have as much pressure to do all and be all. Our way of managing stress is different than men's. In the words of John Grey, women *nest* when they are stressed but men *rest*.

When women are stressed we don't sit down and take a rest or relaxation break; we need to nest, clear our homes, make things neat and pretty, create order and beauty. This is a key understanding about the feminine way. Inactivity doesn't reduce our stress. We need to do something and this requires energy.

Sometimes it is necessary for women to adopt masculine ways but this creates adrenaline in our bodies. When adrenaline persists, women need to refuel through nesting. Understanding this biological need helps us to realize why we are so exhausted. We move most creatively when we feel safe, relaxed and unrushed, when oxytocin is present rather than adrenaline.

In Part Two of the book there are practices that teach you to feel this oxytocin state in your body. We have to remind ourselves what that feels like and bring it into our lives more so we can refuel our bodies. Once we understand on a physical level what this feels like, we can bring more awareness to other techniques that we can use daily to create this calmer state for ourselves. We begin by realizing that we refuel by moving in a relaxed way, unrushed, enjoyably nesting.

I have heard for years about our energy fields. If you study any yoga tradition deeply, energy fields will be addressed. It was head learning for me for many years until I began studying Aharaj yoga. Then it clicked and I understood from a physical perspective what my energy field felt like.

It is a subtle feeling, less perceptible than being touched by someone. It is a clarity that is so small at first that you may miss it but know you feel clearer. All the higher levels of energy and high impressions are like this. You need to fine-tune your perception to notice them. Once you do, the feeling is palpable.

In our classes we always begin with a practice to shift the energy of the group into the present so we can let go of whatever was happening before we arrived. The breathing technique and the movement practice in Part Two will help you learn what a shift in your energy field actually feels like. Feeling a calmer, clearer state to move in is an important part of energy management.

For example, if you noticed that you were in a stressed, scurrying state and then you worked out, moved your body, and increased your oxygen by doing so, you might suddenly feel as though whatever stressed you was no longer a big deal. You created endorphins, moved the energy in your body and created a clearer, calmer, state. You can do this quickly; you don't need an hour workout. Once you notice this shift in your energy, you can find many ways to recreate it.

Your Energy Field

Basically we are each surrounded by our own electromagnetic field. These fields are real; they appear in infrared photos. The field extends out beyond the skin into the air around us. At the end of the day, all our energy is outside our bodies on the perimeter of this field. That is why we are tired and need to rest and rejuvenate.

The key is to have this energy *within* your physical body, operating from your nervous system along your spine. In yoga terms, you need the energy to be within your body in your chakra system. That is why you feel energized when you move, because movement circulates that energy from your outer field and brings it back within your body, resetting your electromagnetic field.

Movement is very important for this reason. I didn't say exercise or working out! Just movement, which is all it takes. Any movement that oxygenates us and circulates the electromagnetic field works to bring more vital energy to us. Paying attention to this subtle field can supply you with more energy for living. Movement can quickly shift you into the present, stop your mind from rambling and get you back into what you are doing.

This is very important. I know multitasking is a way of life for women, yet it drains us to be multi-focused and takes us away from moving creatively. The phrase "do what you are doing" can really help you manage your energy. With only one focus, your energy goes toward the task in a concentrated manner. It's much less draining than trying to operate on many levels at once!

Other Forms of Nourishment

In the nutrition chapter I spoke of three types of nourishment. Nutrition is the first type, the lowest type of energy really, because our bodies use energy to convert food into energy. Eating lighter foods that are easier to digest gives us quicker energy. You can see why eating a full meal is not always the quickest route. How many times do we eat and then want to rest so we can digest? This is not effective energy management.

Oxygen is the next source of nourishment. Belly breathing, working out or taking a walk—all of these oxygenate the body, providing quicker energy than eating. Getting more oxygen helps shift the body's electromagnetic field to create a clearer, more mentally relaxed state because oxygen fuels all of the body functions.

In yoga there is a practice called bellows breathing which involves breathing from your belly like you are a bellows with quick exhales. This can change your feeling of tiredness very quickly because it oxygenates your cells. Our breathing clears 80% of the unwanted substances from our bodies! Deep breathing is a great way to detoxify and reclaim energy.

Lastly, the high impressions are the best energy generators even though they are more subtle. Music is considered a high impression. Think how quickly you start singing and tapping to the beat when an energizing song comes on the radio. This is how high impressions work. Spiritual practices, meditation, inspiring books and people, music, motivational words—these are the high impressions that give you nourishment and energy to move about in a calm, relaxed, powerful state.

How are you using these three types of nutrition? If you consider energy from this standpoint you can see how quickly and easily you can increase your level of energy. Subtle shifts in how you feel can make a huge difference to your whole body as you live and move. Take time to look at your daily tasks and find ways to add these important energy generators into your day, especially when you feel exhausted.

Practicing a ritual in the morning and then going about your day has great benefit but it is more important to notice when you are low and do some practice right then and there to generate energy. That is living yoga— noticing when you need a lift and doing something at that moment to lift you. Managing your energy field in the moment is a lifestyle rather than a scheduled practice.

Personality Types

Another key to generating energy is knowing what type of person you are and how you move through the world. There are three basic planetary types that are taught in Tantric traditions. (Tantra as I have learned is the study of harmonious relationships; the word means *expansion*. Most think that Tantra is a sexual study when in fact sex is just a small part of this tradition.) Tantra is actually about understanding masculine and feminine energy, how they interact, how to create harmony from supposed opposites, and how to blend harmoniously. We all have both feminine and masculine energies and we seek to balance them.

In Tantra, the three basic types of people are *physical, emotional* and *intellectual.* You can notice which type you tend to be and it will help you learn how to motivate and inspire yourself, thus giving you more energy. We each use all three types but one of them is our natural way and it pays to notice this.

A physical person is one who gets energy from moving, from physical activity. When stress happens, physical people need to move, clean the house, work out, run, etc. This gives them balance and helps them to destress. We all get benefits from moving but a physical person uses movement to generate energy and solve problems. If such a person were to take a trip to New York City, they would be interested in experiencing the city physically. They would want to walk, bike, hike through the park, or ice skate at Rockefeller Center.

An emotional person is one who gets energy from strong emotions. They react to stress emotionally—very sad, very happy, moved by the situation from an emotional angle. Emotional people feel compassion and empathy. They want to help save the world; they want everyone to be happy and smiling.

They are powerful in inspiring and affecting others with their emotional vibrations. If an emotional person went to New York, their ideal trip would include seeing the beauty of all the buildings, the colors and people all about, the inspiring art and the lovely fashion on 5th Avenue. All of these things would increase their emotional charge.

An intellectual person is one who gets energy from thinking and reasoning. Intellectual people are inspired by logic and thinking patterns. They consider pros and cons, using reason and facts to make sense of things. They have lots of questions. They are detail-oriented and interested in the reasoning behind things. They like to analyze and digest things in an ordered way.

An intellectual person would experience the city according to a logical plan. They would map out the route, figuring out how to get from one place to another most efficiently to optimize the plan for the whole day, considering where they would eat, what order they would see the sights, and how much money they would need for each event.

You can see how if you went to the city with someone having a different type than you, there could be conflict about how you would explore the city. If you are in a relationship with someone who has a different disposition than you, you know that you are not always in sync. Rarely does anyone embody just one of the three types. We usually have two more dominant types and less of the third.

These basic personality types are a great tool for understanding others and, more importantly, yourself. You are not always the type you think you are either! Take notice of how you automatically react to emergencies or stressful situations. Each type uses a different process to rebalance and reclaim energy for tasks and life. If you are down, knowing which type you are and which path you use to generate energy will help you shift your energy more quickly.

For example, if you are not motivated to do a task and you are intellectual, you use your reasoning and logic to give you the energy to do it. You list all the pros to completing the task, engaging your mental faculties to talk yourself into action. If you are emotional, you create energy by conjuring up heartfelt feelings about helping others, making a difference, anticipating how inspiring and wonderful your world will be if you complete the task. If you are physical, you focus and motivate yourself for the task by moving, exercising, hiking in the woods, cleaning the house, etc.

This is a powerful concept. You are learning how to motivate and inspire yourself with the proper tools that work for you. We are all different and that is why understanding ourselves and what works for us is very important to harmonious living. What works for one doesn't necessarily work for another. Knowing your type and your motivational process will transform your energy and help you motivate, inspire and transform others!

So consider yourself the master of your own energy. You have much to do and your time and energy are finite. Using the strategies in this chapter, practicing expanded nutritional thinking, and moving in a more focused and relaxed way will inspire you and get you excited for life. These simple tools and perspective shifts will align you, providing awareness of your habits and techniques for rebalancing when you feel low. These are important ways to generate vitality and good energy for life.

Lyn Hicks

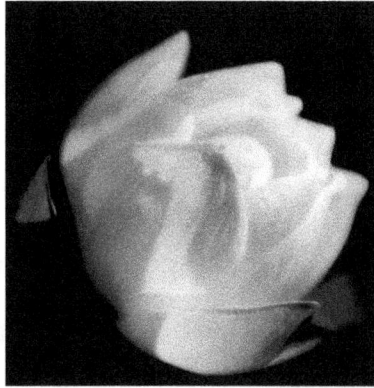

Chapter Ten
Harmonious Relationships

Like the green movement, feminine nature is clearly about creating harmonious relationships with all around us. There is a natural harmony happening already in the universe! The planets orbit slowly and majestically, the balance of light and dark sways each day, the seasons flow into one another, the tides cycle with the moon and all of these affect us. We make choices by tuning into our immediate environments and our thinking is affected by the cycles of life around us.

Once you understand the rhythm and harmony that is all about, that it exists for a reason and there is a set of laws that runs it, it becomes a matter of finding your place in the flow. Nature offers us clear lessons that can greatly enhance our well-being.

Creating relationships that offer a blend of energies, a flow of give and take, a complementary pattern, opens up possibilities. You can accomplish great things in the spirit of cooperation and collaboration. Two can accomplish more than one, and as the numbers increase so does the power of the group.

We are entering into the so-called Aquarian Age where collaboration replaces hierarchy. We see it everywhere as companies join together, as people cross-promote, as Facebook connects so many around the globe. Take time to investigate how you can bring the most to all your relationships so they are positive.

There is great power in numbers, so sharpen your collaborative skills! As women, we are natural collaborators. Reducing the competition between us will bring about a better world. Working with others and using the power of the group inspires our hearts. Women have a larger capacity for communication than men; our brains are designed differently on this front. I'm sure this is no surprise to you!

Tantra Roots

Tantric tradition is a great source of knowledge about harmonious relationships. I was taught that Tantra means *expansion*—expanding through working together. In the modern world, John Grey has demonstrated Tantric principles in a scientific way. When you begin to understand masculine and feminine energy as nature uses them both to create, you find many obvious clues about harmony. Take the bees and the flowers—very different in form and function, one rooted to the spot and one flying about, both helping each other by doing what they do naturally. Truly complementary!

There are two opposing forces operating, a duality. This yin and yang work together to create. A father and a mother make a child. Equal and balanced, the opposites create something new. I see men and women as complementary opposites, creating harmony together. That's how they work in nature.

When you look at the roles of women and men as having general characteristics and you understand the differences, you can blend and create balance in a myriad of ways. You also see things from a natural perspective, so your relationship challenges become focused on integrating energy correctly rather than on personal issues.

Two strong masculine perspectives will butt heads and get into competition, making it more difficult to have a win/win situation. In order to be harmonious, someone has to have the flexibility to allow the blend that is the "child" of the two, the third way. It doesn't matter whether the man or the woman is the blender, or even if they take turns. But there has to be at least one blender for harmony to occur. We all have both feminine and masculine energies and we are to balance them within ourselves first and then with others. Biologically, we are men or women and that is a clue. Understanding the energy of your nature will help you harmonize yourself.

Our hormones and physical characteristics incline our systems to use one of the two energies naturally; the others we grow through consciousness.

Usually it is better for women to use feminine energy and balance it with masculine energy, and for men to use male energy and balance with feminine. So the blend occurs on all levels.

Different Ways of Operating

Men rest when they are stressed and women nest when they are stressed. One sits, the other moves. Women collaborate and talk through problems; men solve them inwardly. Masculine energy is like a straight line from a to b, quick, strategic, ordered, logical, production-oriented, competitive, mechanical, hierarchical and systemic. Thinking is key. Feminine energy is like a curvy line, meandering, enjoying, relaxed, smelling the roses, slower and with a different awareness of what is around us. It is playful, creative, flowing, cooperative, communicative, collaborative. Feelings and emotions are central to feminine energy.

When we tap into the natural feel for ourselves in this blend, we can understand how to make it work better. In order to get along, you have to understand how you balance your partner. It is a lovely study and it can be used in all your relationships.

It is easier to understand the typical feminine and masculine character traits by looking at the extreme versions of each. There is the producer and the one who maintains what is produced, the protector and the protected, the knight and the princess, the provider and the nourisher. It does not matter who plays which role as much as that you grasp that this is the play you are in. These energies must balance to create the optimum blend in a relationship.

When masculine and feminine energy connect in true balance, the blessing is heightened sensuality and complementary energy that feels good and helps you work together smoothly. Whatever way you want to use this, it is high connection! It is easy and flowing; it is that great electric feeling of being in love, in synchronicity, that dreamy energy that creates passion and strong desire on all levels.

Firstly, we must create this balance within ourselves and use self-development to blend our own reasoning and creativity. Both energies want to balance each other naturally within. Once you find the balance that is right for you, you will naturally attract a complementary energy. If you have any unbalance or sense of neediness, a whole slew of obstacles arise. This explains why many relationships do not last.

The second law is that men and women are not meant to be together every minute. We are opposites so in order to keep the energies complementary; we must balance different parts in different ways. Men do their masculine things; women do their feminine things. Each of us is on our own individual mission and path of learning.

When we come together, we do it when we are full of ourselves, high in our respective roles, ready to unite. If one is strong and wanting to connect and the other is not, it is best to stay away from each other or other issues will play out. You can come together if you remember that the balance must exist for connection. The man may take on a nurturing role; the woman may share in strategic thinking. The blend is like a flow between the partners, the energies, and the personalities. You can manage it a million ways as long as balance is the program.

So when a man is in TV mode, he is de-stressing. Don't go at him; he needs to be alone. If a woman is stressed, she should call a girlfriend who likes to communicate or engage in some form of nesting that will create a release. Noticing your own issue allows you to choose the solution.

Men and women will not get everything from each other. They need some separation of their lives and connections to fulfill them completely. Being aware of that and reaching toward balance is better than expecting someone of the opposite energy to "fix" you. As you figure out your way to harmonize, it becomes clear when problems will occur and you learn how to avoid creating negative situations.

I loved learning this. My natural way is more to the extreme feminine traits. The masculine ones of focus I must balance consciously. It doesn't feel natural for me to be efficient, strategic, mathematical, logical. It stresses me when I try to be too task-oriented or production-based the majority of the time. My body feels tense, exhausted and in adrenaline. Of course we all must use masculine energy at times. I use it when I need to, but when it becomes stressful I switch activities to clear and relax my systems. Then I can get back to it if necessary, but I don't force my body to produce cortisol for extended periods of time.

I can also delegate to someone who operates in a more task-oriented way. I am indeed more of a collaborator than a solo creator. Everyone is different. I know that when I am working on a big project, I do best when I cooperate with someone who is more detail-oriented. They share their gifts, I share mine and we both work in our best ways together. Paying attention to your system and knowing how you work best is the key here.

There are many ways to grow and learn once you have awareness.

I feel best living in creative, flowing, and spontaneous ways. Safe, relaxed, open to connecting and communicating, moving at a more meandering pace. Each of us is different and none better than the other. Some women use more masculine energy easily in their unique balance. First we learn to see how we are and how to create a balance within ourselves. Then we can create harmony with others. It is truly about balancing these qualities within and without.

You will naturally find all kinds of mixes. Some women run with strong masculine energy; some men have strong feminine energy. We are all individuals, so the key is to develop your balance and seek support in harmony with others. If you are a strong-willed individual, you may want to mix with a collaborative type; you will connect more easily and harmonize nicely. It is important to notice your natural way.

Many women are using too much masculine energy, forcing themselves into mechanical ways because the world seems to call for it. For most, it is not their natural way. They need to be sure that all sides of themselves are recognized, otherwise they will become exhausted and find themselves with health issues. Staying aware of this has given me great internal understanding and helps me connect well with everyone.

It is not about being weaker than your partner; it is about awareness and solving conflict. It is not about being right, an ego-driven concept; it is about creating peace and harmony. There are times when standing your ground is important but too often we cling to "I'm right and I know it" for things that simply don't matter.

Conflict creates stress and panic in our lives. We need to get back into oxytocin, the relaxed "tend and befriend" mindset. To be fluid and flexible in situations is our natural way. Not to your own detriment, as in letting yourself get pushed around, but in a collaborative way—seeking a greater answer with two minds. Try really grounding yourself in this as a great gift, the magical way you are designed to operate, nourishing and thriving in unison!

Conflict can inspire growth but stress steals your health and vitality. Tend and befriend yourself. Create your own balance within so you feel complete and honored. Then tend and befriend the larger world, not by sacrificing your position but by being balanced and wise, able to adapt your system to an easier, greater way. Let these gifts of understanding carry you into the magical world of harmonious relationships where you can be strong and secure while blending in collaboration. You can shift your position to find a smoother way to create. The Earth is showing us how this is done each day—a loving study in living!

Chapter Eleven
Sacred Femininity

Sacred femininity—what does that mean? To honor the feminine principle as sacred, equal, and different. To realize that femininity's harmonizing, collaborative way is powerful in its flexibility. It is opposite of and complementary to masculine power. Not thinking only with the mind, but feeling, intuitive, sensing with a deeper part of ourselves and creating balance.

Feminine essence is the core of our power and it does not come through the mind. It is a gift. It offers a different model of being that is more than just thinking, and it can only operate when we are connected to our bodies, to the gut feeling where intuition is housed. We all have a mix of masculine and feminine energy. As women we are centered in the feminine and balance with the masculine. Feminine spirit is creative, sensual, collaborating, connecting, sexual in nature.

I am speaking of the traits that make us leaders. We deeply unite and connect with people, inspire others, motivate, nourish, communicate, solve problems, intuit and cooperate. These are the expressions of our sexual, creative nature, our feeling way that we perceive the world. This is the energy we need to nurture and use, and we start by inspiring and delighting ourselves.

The basic chakra system of yoga defines seven chakras, some masculine and others feminine. Chakras are junction points in your body that regulate energy between the metaphysical and physical worlds. They are located on your spine and they affect your central nervous system. The feminine chakras are the second (Svadhisthana) chakra, located below the belly at the womb, the fourth (Anahata) chakra in the area of the heart, and the fifth (Visuddha) chakra, which is in the area of the throat. The first (Muladhara) chakra, at the root of your spine toward the Earth, the third (Manipura), above your belly button and the sixth (Ajna), between your eyebrows are male.

The male traits have to do with physical and mechanical workings. They are action-oriented through competition, focus, strategic planning and organization. They define the forms of things that will come into being. We all have a measure of these important traits. The order of the world is based on these male qualities, but today there is too much of this in women's lives. If we are over weighted in mechanical, organizational tasks, we become apathetic and uninspired because we are not using all of our energy centers correctly.

My message is that we are spending too much time in non-feminine roles, neglecting our feminine spirit which is the dynamic part of the universe— changing, flowing, shifting, never the same. The Svadhisthana chakra is creative and fun. Like water it reminds us to flow with life situations, relationships, communication and flexibility. Like bamboo it shows us how to bend with the wind.

Our youthful way comes from this center. The kidneys are there to regulate the water in our bodies. We are 70% water so it pays to understand how this flowing affects our bodies! The heart (Anahata) chakra deals with worldly love and deep feelings, engaging our emotions to manifest ideas that will make a difference in the world. Our souls and hearts need to be inspired!

The Visuddha chakra is the center of creativity and individuality. It is home to the voice, a woman's rhythmic voice that speaks kindly and creates new ideas. Collaborative and friendly, women are students and open communicators. We are negotiators and problem solvers, using our connections with others to create win/win situations.

These traits must be nurtured to help balance a woman's life. Developing these gifts can inspire us and keep us lively and creative, motivated by our ideas and energized for all our tasks, male or female. Are these areas balanced in your life? How do you inspire and motivate yourself?

Self-Care

We must understand the importance of caring for ourselves. We have been told to take care of ourselves for years, yet we don't act on this advice! Without time to inspire ourselves, to tap into our creative joy and build relationships with ourselves, we become depressed or ill. We may have some success but without nurturing our own feminine energy we will turn apathetic, unfocused, unbalanced, and we will be unable to proceed in beauty and vitality.

The need to care for ourselves first and create balance on all levels is the most important tip that this book offers. Women are artists and our chakras are energy centers that offer us fuel to move about the world and create.

Most of women's problems come from operating with too much adrenaline, which creates cortisol in our bodies and causes us to become unbalanced. We have problems with our wombs, hearts, breasts and voices. It is scientific knowledge that these are common health issues for women.

The amount of cortisol in our systems is killing us. Why? Because we are in fight or flight mode too much of the time, scurrying from task to task in a panic. As women, our biochemistry operates best when we are out of the sympathetic nervous system of adrenaline and in the parasympathetic nervous system of oxytocin. If we continue to exhaust our bodies this way, we will be in biochemical health crisis.

We create when we are in safety, in a relaxed state of doing, when the hormone oxytocin is present. How often is that? Not nearly enough, so it makes sense that we have these health issues. We must begin to spend time with ourselves, grounded into our bodies, nourishing and inspiring ourselves first in order to overflow into the world. It must become a priority. We are striving for a more peaceful life, a slower pace and a richer experience. These are feminine ways.

I study and teach about the movement for women to reclaim our place as co-creators. Our nurturing nature needs to expand. We need to be educated on how to nourish ourselves, how to avoid feeling depleted, how to refuel for all our tasks. Playing the exhausted caregiver is aging us so. Learning more about the female body, the way it moves and my own energy helped me align myself to be more balanced in these areas in my life.

In Part Two of this book, I share some practices for reconnecting with your body, your beauty, your Shakti energy. Other cultures of ancient times educated women and girls about their femininity—how to care for their wombs, connect with nature, practice ways to be more flowing and move like a woman. There were exercises to open and honor parts of their bodies, discussions on health, movement, charm, sensuality, dancing and singing. They honored their differences from men, their ability to collaborate and balance their communities.

From a biological standpoint, we are the greatest creators here on the planet at this time. We can create new life! Think of how many of us, myself included, somehow got the message that we were not creative. It is such an oxymoron! Our biology, our hormones and organs, our systems are designed to bring about new life.

How could we get so disconnected from ourselves and our bodies that we would believe we have no creativity? We create so many wonderful things—beautiful homes, wonderful food, great relationships among people of different dispositions. We build communities and support systems through schools, workplaces and neighborhoods; we even create our own unique look and style.

Truly we are great creators in a soft, nurturing way. The kindness we offer others day in and day out needs to be turned in on ourselves. We need to connect to ourselves, our female bodies, and our power as creators. Release the thinking that suggests otherwise; it simply is not true. It is based on old cellular memories as well as the misinformation found in our current society. Inequality has done enough damage; we must reclaim our beauty to shift the balance back toward equality. We must claim equality inwardly, knowing that we offer balance to the world with our lovely collaborative, creative ways.

Nurturing your feminine spirit and strengthening those qualities is fun, natural and fulfilling! It is also simple and quick. It is not something to force upon yourself, like many beliefs today. Getting healthier doesn't have to be drudgery. Feminine practices are fun and easy.

It seems too simple, but our bodies are *designed* to operate in a more playful, emotional way. When we allow ourselves to do this we become giddy with joy, teenagers with the giggles. We are not designed to be so serious and intellectual the way men are. Our way is lighter, more joyous, more perceptive in feeling and being.

Lyn Hicks

Women's Leadership

Woman leaders operate on different principles than men. We are less formal in our leadership and we have deeper connections with those who work with us. We are motivators; we love inspiration and we need to be connected deeply to our roles and tasks. Our roles draw on our hearts and our nurturing natures, and they fuel our being.

Feminine characteristics often fall to the wayside in this male-oriented world. Women will find more vitality and passion when we nurture our creativity first. It is time; it is necessary; it is fun and rewarding. When we embrace ourselves and show up to the workplace in full equal power, using our femininity rightly and strongly in business, a lot of the world's problems will move toward solution.

As the Dalai Lama says, Western women will help the world. When women have money and power, when we use our nurturing way in business, we will help all women toward basic rights. Businesses will care about the environment and make sure the land and resources are used to benefit all. We naturally do these things in our small worlds; we can transcend differences and see the world as one family.

I have spoken of this feminine principle in so many ways and I hope you find yourself seeking deeper nourishment for your unique exquisite expression as a woman. All the chapters in this book speak to your feminine side. Eat nourishing food, create a sacred home space, try heartfelt spiritual thinking, connect with others through inspiration and support. Use nature's creative energy and learn about holistic healing which gets to the deeper root of illness with fun tools and medicines. Practice artistic environmentalism, energy management, harmonious relationships and choices in vibrant living with vital energy. These are creative, playful ways to move in the world, our sacred femininity.

We are creatives; we are artists; we are inspired by these things. In balancing ourselves we will lead our families, our communities and the whole world into balance. It is the call of our times. It is the energy shift we are moving into. It is beautiful and lovely that we can begin to balance the whole of our existence by balancing our feminine spirit. We have suffered and been martyred enough.

It is time to begin the Lotus Project. To awaken the true feminine power that nourishes us and, through us, nourishes all those around us. With our leadership, the world will be a more inspiring place to create. Our joy will grow large, our laughter will grow louder! On all levels, our systems will be nourished and able to operate at their best. We need to cultivate feminine culture as they did in ancient times, when the goddesses inspired people to create more connected ways of being. It is our time, it is our purpose, and our lives will be deeply affected as we evolve through this great experience on Earth!

Empathic Awareness

This is a topic I could write a whole book about and indeed just may one day. Woman are naturally empathetic. We easily and most naturally feel others emotions. This is our gift of sensing so to speak. We all have some sort of 6th sense that allows us to feel the world in a different way than just seeing what is about and thinking a conclusion. It is part of our intuition and why we are the nourishers and birth humanity as it moves forward. This is the gift of our feminine essence.

We naturally feel how our kids are doing. We notice who needs help, who is sick, who is angry, who needs support. It is part of our physical and emotional make up as woman. It is not a thinking, it is an awareness on another level. Some woman are really sensitive and tapped into this consciously, others are not. It is a gift to us all and available to us to notice and develop. If we are connected to our bodies, really sunk into them, then this power can be used more consciously. If we are only in our thinking mind having that run our beness, we are cut off from this sensing because it comes as a gift of our body not mind.

This is part of the discovery I am learning as I complete this book. Exactly how this gift operates so naturally within woman. I believe we are uneducated about this sensing nature and in ancient feminine cultures this was clearly understood, taught about and consciously developed. It is the sacred feminine essence that has hidden power within us that we are not tapping properly. As I do the practices I share in this book, as I learn to be more relaxed throughout my life, I find this gift unfolding rapidly and easily.

It is what gives us our sense of connectedness to the world. We naturally have this ability and understanding of our connection to others. We truly feel the group energy, we sense the flavor of environments, we have a deep knowing we are all connected on a level different than the mind. It is just a knowing that eludes the mind often and why we question it rather than develop it. I know you all know what I am speaking of even if my words don't describe it well.

As I speak with woman, grow my community on this deeper level, I find all woman have this 6th sense. Some people connect with nature, hear the messages, understand her in a myriad of ways. Some woman feel others, they just know what is going on without words if one is in a good or bad state. Others see auras, colors about people, sense in a visual way. Some sense spirits of people passed about and get messages that way. Some hear wisdom from somewhere and just know to share what they hear with others. We get gut feelings, not to go somewhere or to call someone. This is the gift of sacred femininity. This is our essence that goes untapped.

These sensings are very real and our gift as woman. This whole craft of understanding the world from an energetic, connected way is part of our being that knows the world differently than thinking and must be developed to truly be our authentic selves.

My journey with empathy has been fraught with misunderstanding. As I learn to connect with my body and sink into it, feeling it's messages, I realize I have misused this gift and actually misunderstood the world around me. I am certain many other woman have this very challenge because it is part of who we are, this sensing.

I believe it has so much to do with our flowing feelings and how we are misunderstanding these gifts thus considered erratic and unstable. Often this instability of our feelings rides us into exhaustion when it is more of a guiding mechanism gone amuck. Men have this sense as well. Remember all have masculine and feminine within us and must balance these opposites.

My daughter gifted me the Goddess Oracle, deck and book set by Amy Sophia Marashainsky for my birthday this past year. I was most interested in the lovely pictures and wanted to see woman role models. I alone could not think of 52 feminine qualities that should be cultivated. As I pulled the cards, played with them and offered them to my friends and students, a huge awakening came forward.

I realized these archetypes, these Goddessses from all cultures and regions, were describing our vast emotional nature. They seemed to represent feelings, different states of the wave we are riding and explained them as a guidance system, something to notice. Seeing these beautiful images describing things like nourishment, wisdom, beauty, fear, doubt, victimhood, sensuality, wild woman, mystery, anger, justice, pleasure, awakened a knowing in me of my feeling nature. It allowed me the perspective to see this feeling nature as a guidance system rather than letting it run me.

As I begin to understand the guidance they offer me, consciously recognizing my feelings for the message rather than getting out of them, I find more power in them and how to allow them to exist without going into the emotion of them. Feelings are the sensing, telling me about the world around me. Maybe one is unkind and I feel hurt. The message here is to notice and move away and disconnect. Our reaction to feelings is our emotion. Energy moving is how I describe emotion. So I feel hurt and now my reaction is to call up other times I felt hurt. I start thinking how this has happened in the past, I remember other situations and now I have energy moving and thinking of all this pain. This is misuse of our guidance system. I believe it is why our emotional nature has such a negative connotation to it. Our emotions are riding us rather than be the gift of awareness they are.

Feeling Others

The other most important learning I have discovered through all this study is that I deeply feel others state of feeling. I have always deeply felt others and just operated with it unknowingly. I never quite understood it when I was young, the taking in of others emotions. It just happened, I had no understanding of it, I just felt others. We all do this naturally. I would mold and bend myself to smooth out those emotions. If there is tension in a group, I will become the energy that is needed to resolve the conflict, shift the perspective, try to blend the group to a happier situation. We do this while raising children very wonderfully. Sensing our child's feelings and then try to shift them back to joy.

The issue that has tripped me up about all this was that I was not consciously separating my feeling from that of others. So I would leave a situation a lot less energized than when I went. I would feel someone's sadness, their strife or struggle so deeply as though it was mine quite naturally. I would take it in and try to shift it. When I do this, now I have ones low feeling that naturally calls up a matching feeling in my life. I empathize, put myself in their shoes. By doing this I feel a time in my life when I felt that feeling to relate to them. This is where we misuse our gift. The moment we go deeply into another's feelings.

We get to choose how deeply we feel others. If my friend has cancer it is a huge challenge. I lost my dad to cancer. In speaking with her in an unaware state of empathy, I would begin to call up all the pain and strife of watching my dad live and die with cancer. This is where I have gone over the line of using my empathy wisely. Now I am in some deep emotion. It could be considered a very low vibration of helplessness. Is this what my friend needs me to do to support her? Not at all.

What I need to do here is realize that my friend is in challenge. I empathize and have compassion because I have dealt with this issue of cancer before. Putting down my gift of empathy I move to compassion which allows me to see her strife with no judgment and just love. She needs courage, love and openness. I offer her the understanding and bear witness to her challenge. I do not need to go deeply into my feelings that I had when my dad died. I chose to understand her and reflect what is needed from that more neutral loving place.

This is a very important distinction and understanding for woman. Naturally we often just connect with another and feel their feelings intensely. We don't offer the proper support or understand that this empathy is to know who and what needs our love and compassion. We don't need to ride their emotions, we need to be there offering a higher vibration of love and support. That is why we have this gift. To connect, collaborate and support the world rightly. Using our sensing mechanism to see where the nurturing and nourishing is necessary.

I missed this lesson and am discovering how to use our flow, our feeling cyclical nature to understand the world about me. Not to be ridden by the many feelings and messages about me that are filling me up.

I was allowing this sensitivity to others run amuck and overwhelm me to be considered a crazy woman as they say. If misunderstood or stuffed away or talked or thought out of our feelings, they become powerful emotions and can explode in havoc. Kali, the Goddess who could kill her world in her trance like dance of fear and death. What woman has not had those moments? It is part of our nature to understand and balance these feelings of ourselves, our feeling of others.

This lead me to start to notice others feelings from my own. Wow was this huge! I began to realize I could really feel others in a deep way. I began realizing I would leave someone and their feeling would now be mine. Part of my being, my field of existence. This was a huge understanding because I had confused myself and my own feelings and energy. I was not able to tell my feelings from others. Where was Lyn's feelings? What were they?

It all blended and I was in emotion. So I would try to move negative feelings that were about me, using techniques and tips of my mental mind to shift my direction and be in charge of my life. I would try them, seemed logical but they did not work. I know what I need to do always by now in most situations with health and wellbeing yet I do not do them.

Doing the exercises in the book, looking at the world in a more heart felt way has caused this learning to come forward. Yes silly to dance, to step into my feelings, to honor myself first, to enjoy being a woman, nourish my body with coconut oil and pretty make up. To buy things luxurious for my family knowing it is the best available to build our home and environment we live, to giggle and laugh, consider the world magical through sound and music, through eating consciously and making my tasks a pleasure through presence. All this information has opened me up to my empathic awareness of the world about me in a deeper way.

I call it a 6th sense. We all have it and we are now being called to develop it. This has been my learning from studying ancient feminine cultures, woman's story and cycle in the world. We were the healers and the nourishers. We have a sense of connectedness to the world like mother nature does to the diverse kingdom she is part of. Using this seasonal, cyclical nature seems to me to be speaking of our emotions. Our feeling way.

To develop this as our gift, to ride the cycle of dynamic movement and understand the feeling intuitive, flowing existence we experience seems the call of our feminine culture. Knowledge of our feeling nature, the depths of it, the guidance of it, the wisdom of it is found through grounding into your body and honoring the creative essence you are.

As I have danced and grounded into my body. I have realized that I am my own space of being. I have a field about me that I have sovereignty over. It is my space and being that I bring to a situation. Lyn alone with her space. I get a chance to feel myself fully in joy, in devotion, in gratitude. I feel good. I like myself and body. I sink into it.

Aharaj has taught me that I have sanscords or energetic connections to memories, people, places with in me that connect out to things outside me and many of these are draining my energy field. So I learn to be conscious of this space and use the negative stress and strife in life to transform that through conscious expression. Feeling the power of those stress emotions as I get them out of my field. I must be in charge of my space.

Lyn Hicks

The breathing has taught me what I feel like in a relaxed state, something I forgot. I learned to consciously bring a shift in my body, my feeling nature to make it cozier and more in pleasure. To remember that feeling of pleasure, of good vibe.

I have learned many other practices of Tai Chi health movements and ways of the woman in the ancient cultures. They did the things we liked to do but knew the power of it. This gathering to of woman in a Red Tent seemed to have Harem feeling to it. I love that thought of being part of a group of beautiful woman, flourishing, dancing, giggling and enjoying themselves in a luxuriously, sensuous way.

Doing things that promote generating high emotions help train your body to naturally do that for you. This is harnessing the emotional nature. Then seeking to understand the guidance of our emotions to see what they are telling us so we may fluidly flex about like water, flowing through our feelings. Because of our natural gifts we have, each of us different in how we sense the world with our feeling nature, we must learn to know our own space of ourselves. This is what we are missing as woman.

The ability to just be ourselves in our own space. We have sensed so many things in many ways inexplicable. It is just natural for us to be connected to others. At this point that is what I am learning regarding my power as a woman. Learning to feel Lyn, just me and what I feel has been the learning. In this there has been a great power awakened with in. I call this Shakti. A knowing of myself as queen of my dominion of energy and space. I enjoy generating my own good feelings and then heading out into the world only allowing in what nourishes me. Not only that but savoring the nourishment already about me that I must just slow down to partake of.

Sacred Femininity to me is developing this 6th sense as woman together. Each sharing our development, gathering nourishing each other in a very real way, consciously, passionately, deliciously, so we can collaborate beautifully. Supporting the production, the things we are creating on this earth by adding a woman's heart to everything. This is the essence of being a woman. Using your magical power to support the world uniquely and beautifully. Power and softness in only the way of a woman.

All of this information you have heard before on so many levels. I hope the way I put these ways of living together you can see things in a fun, exciting way, this movement we are part of and can only say 'thus I have heard" and we then experiment with what we have learned. I have done these things and treated life and myself in a more honorable way. I am learning ways to feel that deeply.

Yes, I go through life with crisis always about. Learning to be conscious and generate a high state in your body of health requires a conscious effort. Honoring myself, my sensuality, my spirit, I have begun to awaken my gift more fully of my 6th sense. It is tied to me understanding my emotions being indicators and how to separate them from others. It is a delightful process and I invite you to engage.

Live in your body, it is a wonderful mechanism we have been bestowed. It is sacred and we need to honor it. When we do, it begins to work for us as a tool of awareness to the world about us in a more subtle way. We must slow down to notice, we must be perceptive at a subtler level. Feelings are quick and moving, energy gliding about. Using this sense rightly and with mindfulness seems to be a great power we must develop.

To be in the pleasure of the moment is the gift of presence. Presence, being where we are when we are there, is the key to creativity. Sinking into my senses and noticing the wonder of being sensual with them, has developed a relaxation in my body. From there I can be the most present, open to the infinite possibility available in the moment. This seems to be the way to be in joy in the moment. I find my body a great way to bring me to presence. The sensing feeling nature I have is a gift to explore.

I inspire you to investigate the gift of your feeling, sensing side. This has power and wisdom to it when understood. Our feelings need to be understood as indicators. A sensing of the world. To use this consciously toward the good of all is the unfolding of our gift of feminine essence. How do we elevate this sensing as a high feminine quality, filled with knowledge to help the world? This is the shift I am part of and want to inspire. I want everyone to bloom and shine and exude their wonderfulness. Only then will the garden of the world flourish. When we all grow together at different paces, times and cycles.

I have lots of energy and can use it against myself if I do not pay attention. That is why my look at the world has to do with energy management. It has been my learning to try to understand it so I can use it rightly rather than in idle doing.

From here I will continue as a student in life, learning how to harness my feeling gift. May we all do this sacred act of honoring our feelings and self properly so we may change the world into a more connected place. The green movement, the local movement, the woman's movement all have the same flavor of nourishing here and now, who we are and where we live. That begins in our hearts, in our feeling nature where we want the good of all to reign.

However you can cultivate this awareness in yourself to me seems the worthy next step in our journey as blossoms. Truly understanding our hearts, opening them as the lotus opens its golden center to the sun. Harnessing this feeling nature to elevate it to the dynamic flow it is. That seems to me to be the opening of the heart of our femininity. This is the knowing that is unfolding within me. May we learn this together and create a strong community by educating and learning about ourselves by deciphering this feeling way. Each of us sharing our way we do it and weaving it with others.

For Lyn's Take on Our
Empathetic Nature, visit
www.LotusProjectBook.com

A Feminine Community

I host a growing group of women who come together to learn these traditions and teachings. I find this study experiential. It is not just women in business, girls networking their crafts or gathering for cocktails and venting. It involves conscious development of our minds, bodies, hearts and spirits.

Women need to learn about their centers of power and the feminine gifts that flow through them. We need to open ourselves to becoming more fulfilled, healthier and thus more helpful. When we gather we need to get out of our thinking minds and into our hearts, not venting but building ourselves in support of who we want to become. We can strengthen our gifts by speaking of ways to become more balanced, more present, more joyous.

You can find out more on my blogs or join my mailing list at harmonyhillgardens.com to receive information. As I learn, I will teach and share what I know with all who want to learn. Gathering and discussing our deeper problems about how to fill and nourish ourselves, how to take time to honor ourselves and our connection to our bodies. Moving in a more relaxed way, safe, creative in all we do, sensual and soft, playful and passionate, open and flexible, using our hearts and our sweetness.

Our next step is to raise the feminine vibe together in unison with others. Join us as we help balance the world!

Chapter Twelve
Modern Femininity

When we were teenagers gathered at slumber parties, something important was happening in our bodies as the female hormones rushed in. Its mystery was and is a secret to us—we knew a change was happening, but we received so little guidance from our society, our moms, and our schools.

The way we approach girls' transition to maturity is anything but delightful. The information we receive is basic and the secret of our intuition is still hidden. Other cultures have honored this as such an important transitional time. We have lost the traditions of the gift of this cycle. It is one of the first transitions into womanhood and somehow its meaning, the beauty and power of it, goes unnoticed.

Most of us don't really know what to make of it. We were not taught about the wonder of this transition and neither were our mothers. The lack of education and honor leads to a disconnection from our bodies that clearly begins at this time. Our bodies begin to grow and change, we gather in fun and beauty and then our cycles begin. There is no sense of beauty and honor associated with it—instead we think of emotional instability and discomfort.

This new body and its cycle become a hassle, a hindrance to being and doing. The culture around menstruation has become dismal and this fundamental piece of the life cycle is used against us. Just as we are learning to love our developing bodies, we are "plagued" with our cycle, which will bring years of moodiness and dismay, even pain. How can we not disconnect from our bodies?

The Red Tent

There is an ancient tradition of women called the Red Tent. In the old days, when women got their cycles it was a time for them to step away from their normal chores and communities. They went to the Red Tent, which was filled with other women. They communed only with women because their bodies were in a powerful state of release.

It was considered a precious time. They were not ostracized because they were unclean, they were set apart because the cycle of life was flowing through them. Their bodies were renewing as they did monthly. It was the time of their flow.

Women looked forward to this time of enjoying and nurturing each other in the Red Tent. It was natural and relaxing. Good food, compassionate care and nurturing were bestowed upon them as they rested, taking a reprieve from everyday life and allowing their bodies to rejuvenate the life-giving cycle. They moved slower, they played about, they honored their bodies, they enjoyed the inward movement towards themselves and their needs.

They knew that this flowing way was a gift—the emotional nature, the flow of feeling energy, a cycle of release and rest for their bodies that had everything to do with being a woman. It was honored and given its place in life. This cycle was their gift of sensitivity and intuitive nature, not just physically with the blood but socially with the way women move and work with others. We are meant to flow with life and with each other. Women who hang together naturally harmonize and they begin to get their cycles at the same time.

Each month we are reminded of our flowing nature. A flow is a cycle like a wave. It has an ebbing way, power on one end and rest at the other. It is how we move. It is the cycle of life in our bodies and the cycle of emotion that runs our intuition. This is a gift that women naturally have, a rhythm like the seasons in nature.

By not honoring this cycle, we don't honor the way we should work with ourselves and our flowing feminine nature. We try to fit into a masculine way of production and order, but being in high gear 30 days a month defies the rhythm of our bodies. We are not systematic and stable in that way; we are rhythmic and fluid in a different way. Our beat is more syncopated, like music for dancing as opposed to marching.

This is life flowing through women. Our bodies tell us our way—more relaxed at times, more powerful at other times. We need to remember this gift of our feeling nature. Because of our disconnection from our bodies we have not harnessed the power of our feeling, shifting way and it often controls us erratically. We should be noticing this cycle and our feelings so we know where we are in the wave.

We are the dynamic creativity of the universe, ever changing and shifting. We have missed this key to our nature. We naturally flow in a cycle and we need to use this to our advantage. In honoring ourselves and our rhythms we can begin to honor the cycles around us in nature, giving us a deeper connection to the Earth and ourselves as an intricate part of it.

Youth-Building Playfulness

The great unconscious wonder of our bodies shares its gifts with young girls. As their hormones rush in, we can watch their natural way, the things they do and see how their bodies direct them before they disconnect.

As girls, we gathered together, we danced seductively, naturally feeling our bodies change. We had no understanding yet our bodies wanted to move in this sensual way. We dressed up, painted our nails, put on makeup and fed ourselves; we giggled and did silly girl things until all hours of the night. We were so delighted; we had so much fun and were nourished on many levels without even being aware of it.

Just watching how girls have fun together at a slumber party is so telling. This is the natural beginning of the Red Tent. It is just what girls do, taking care of ourselves and each other. This nurturing fun is key to our femininity and to building the connection with our bodies.

We see evidence of this throughout our lives. What do we want to do when we get together? Dance! Most girls go out all decked to the nines with the goal to dance. We are prettied up and out on the town enjoying ourselves for ourselves. Our goal is to have fun and be giddy and joyous, youthful and carefree.

This is very telling about feminine culture and how we create blessing for each other, how we create energy to enjoy ourselves and love ourselves. It has nothing to do with men. Yes, it is lovely to get their attention now and then but it is not the real goal. Competing for them or against each other is not our natural way—we would rather just have fun.

We celebrated our femininity when we were young as it came upon us with new hormones, feelings and curves. We liked to make ourselves feel beautiful and charming, sensuous and playful, pulsing with the energy of being a girl. We celebrated our bodies joyfully. This is how we loved ourselves and our femininity.

As adults, we gather at spas to rest and relax together. We get our nails done and commune with other women beautifying themselves; we get massages and other nourishing treatments. We come together with food and everyone adds to the meal. These are the ways of the Red Tent and important keys to our feminine nurturing. These days no one has time to do this anymore. Maybe once a year? How can we honor our bodies and understand our flow without giving them attention?

Notice how we offer love to each other and ourselves as we gather. Connecting to ourselves, our bodies and our intuitive nature seems forefront. We must reclaim our feeling ways. The positive effects of our gatherings will be reduced if we don't realize that those teenage activities—dancing, feeling love and honor for our femininity, our curves, and our sensuality—are the ones that strengthen our connection to our bodies and our intuitive centers.

Practicing consciously how we move and why we are different, honoring our fluidity, flexibility, and sensuality connects us to our essence. This may seem silly or simple but it has such power. We naturally desire this. Unfortunately for many of us, religious doctrines and upbringing make it seem inappropriate, unconstructive, or even immoral. These blocks to self-love are deep and must be opened for us to access this power. Our sensitivity to others, our passion and our feeling nature awakens with much strength when it is honored and valued, not in a sexual way but in a sensual way.

Self-love stirs the power of Shakti, the feminine essence within us. Practices to increase self-love and femininity are fun and playful. They are easy for women to do; our bodies naturally want to move gracefully and be honored. It is not a "have to" program like so many of our current health and fitness strategies. These easy practices build oxytocin in the body as we move in joy the way our bodies were meant to move. This power manifests quickly as we connect to it and we find a well of inner energy we didn't know existed. Our intuitive nature awakens and we start to feel more settled in ourselves.

When you feel more at home in your own skin, you don't need so much advice and support, for you feel that you have tapped into a source of discernment and knowledge that you can use to solve problems and support yourself in your own individuality. It is magnificent! Maybe these playful ways are not quite what you would expect but they are very powerful and natural.

I like to learn while having fun. Being too serious takes the passion out of life. You could try to love yourself through mental ways; you could feel the deep pain within emotionally until it releases or you could just gather with others and enjoy being women. Gathering achieves the same end quicker. Yes, sadness may move through but there is support in the group so it quickly turns to laughter. This is certainly an easier way to release the cellular memory of all the negative training women have received!

This is a huge key to building feminine community—gathering together in a more playful way, knowing that we create together in collaborative energy. We are not meant to be so ordered, task-driven and strategic all day long. We get things done from a more magical view when we gather, have fun, and build ourselves and each other by holding this space of creation, then join our lovely forces together in a dance. We dance in artistry, flowing in the swirling energy of playfulness and heartfelt action, moving towards what we want to be and create.

Even the planning becomes a delightful mix of talents and everything gets done with the group members' gifts. The more the better, the easier, and the less work for each person. Building feminine communities in this way will shift things quickly because it allows us to use our flowing, flexible nature together in a way that is natural for us. This is Tantra, the creation of harmonious relationships of expansion. It even explains why men love to look at groups of women—because we are graceful and beautiful when we create together! There is a dance, an art, a soft magic that productivity alone cannot achieve. It is our power. It is what is needed to balance the way of things.

Proudly, my sister and I have naturally done this with our nieces and daughters. As they have grown up we have delighted in getting beautiful together, sharing clothes, helping each other look good by doing make up and clothes. There is 7 of us and at our gatherings over the summer and at the holidays, we revel in getting ready sometimes to do nothing really. We are all packed in the bathroom seeking room to beautify, giddy and helpful and inspired by each other. We think we all look good in our unique ways and strengthen that in our gatherings.

One year we got all decked out for New Years and after our family dinner we loaded in the car and drove down to my sister's beach house in Long Beach Island. Our ages not permitting us all in bars but we left at 10 and figured we would ring the year in there. As midnight struck, we were on the bridge to the island and pulled over the car, no one was on the road, blared the music and danced in the moonlight on the breezy bridge! We giggled and danced, screamed and were full of our wonder. One of my great fun memories of our times and we just had each other, our beauty and the lovely nature filled us all that night of esteem, magnificence and our beautiful selves! We have naturally done this and it has been so fun for us all! It is because it is the way we need to be to empower each other in our uniqueness, just natural.

Universal Energy

We are the collaborators, the tenders of the community, the Girl Scouts, the PTA, the sources of support on all levels. These are very purposeful roles, of course—even more so when you look at the energetic level. Gathering for a higher purpose and working in unison toward a more beautiful world generates great universal energy. We create what they call an aggregor in Aharaj Yoga, a circle of loving energy that builds and supports. This is our feminine power.

This universal energy source we tap into contains the important lost wisdom of women. When we gather in gossip, to vent and complain about our lives, we use this energy to keep ourselves down, stuck in the very situations we are seeking to change. The communal energy is used to strengthen our weaknesses and problems. Its true power and purpose is to be used in development and nurturing ourselves and others to as we gather and share our goals, our visions, our becoming.

This is the power of women in community and in conscious development—a power easily reclaimed once we know of it. The universal power and energy is there awaiting us, and the empowerment we can claim through using it rightly will change ourselves and the world.

These are ideas to begin building our feminine culture so it offers the best to us and other women. Uniting our efforts to create a more magical world, gathering playfully to build ourselves, we can share this evolved way with younger girls as they step into womanhood. Their natural behavior tells us about ourselves! Uniting and supporting each other in all ways, sharing in community and dispelling the competition between us, we can all be beautiful side by side. We can all share our unique gifts in the dance of collaboration!

Chapter Thirteen
Alluring Beauty

We see the essential nature of something—a flower, some art, a person—
and we call it beautiful. We take a moment to breathe in the experience of
that thing. That moment is one of honor and reverence. It is a vibration, a
sense of awe, not just a mental process. We luxuriate in the feeling of this
experience for a moment.

This is different than the models of beauty we have in our society. We are
told to be this or that is to be beautiful. Yet when we experience beauty it
is not just subjective. It is something that catches our eye and makes us
feel, makes us stop what we are doing and just take it in for a moment.
Let's look at beauty this way.

When I go to the garden, it has many colors and textures, many modes
of beauty. Some I like; others are not for me, but to someone else they
appear lovely. So we begin by remembering that beauty is in the eye of the
beholder. You are the beholder. You behold what you find beautiful and it
is different for each of us.

How do we bring this idea of beauty towards ourselves? We must see
our own beauty first before it vibrates authentically to others. We begin
by finding the special traits in ourselves that we find lovely. We all
have things we like about ourselves, we just need to focus on them and
accentuate them. See them as gifts of beauty that you alone share with the
world. Honor yourself by choosing to behold what you like about yourself.

All of us have a list of a few things that are beautiful about ourselves, perhaps our lovely eyes or our shapely legs. What else is there? The way we care for others? The way we help our families? The kindness we offer? The support we give our friends? We begin with this list of what we find beautiful in ourselves.

How do we bring this inward? We revel in it. We accentuate it. We honor it for a moment. We take time to allow that good feeling to vibrate within. That is how it starts, the awestruck feeling of "I wouldn't want to be anybody else." This is our work and our development of beauty—finding our own ways, looks, and actions that we consider beautiful.

You are a flower in your own uniqueness. To feel this, to sink into the gifts you have and develop them is to become beautiful. Throughout this book I have encouraged you to remember the artist you are, an intuitive being who is feeling your way through life. Reminding you to sink into your body, your womb, and your feeling nature is the point of these chapters. In doing so your beauty unfolds.

The green movement offers a wonderful opportunity for us to value and honor ourselves through the choices we make. In doing so, as we move about with more inspiration in our hearts, our choices are wiser and healthier. We honor ourselves by living this way so our beauty shines naturally.

Feminine Community

Our society offers us mixed messages on beauty. How can we hold ourselves to be magnificent with these images of glamour everywhere? That is where our feminine culture comes in and we develop our beauty together. Our emotional nature is most nurtured by women. Women help us understand ourselves as we learn to ride the wave of life. When we gather in joy, knowing that we support each other in living, we naturally complement and reflect beauty in each other. This builds us tremendously—not in a competitive way, but in a collaborative way. Feeling good and powerful as a woman beautifies and enhances everything about us!

Relaxation, oxytocin, and creative fun call us from deep within. This joy that we conjure together is like a health serum. Our systems flood with collaboration, flexibility, and giggliness. We move and play and fill our bodies with oxygen together. We dance, we feel safe and creative, we switch to the parasympathetic nervous system and let our hair down. This is what women need for beauty. It is magnetizing, alluring, and magical.

We apply face masks, we do yoga, we practice movements for our hips, we remind ourselves with oils and soaps and potions that we are women. We make luscious foods and drinks. We share health and shopping tips and ways to be more stunning. These acts add to our beauty. Doing them together has an even greater effect. We become beautiful creators, reflecting our magnificence to each other. We help each other see ourselves through eyes of love. We suggest ways to wear our hair, our clothes, and this adds a glow to our being.

Delighting in feminine ways together creates beauty. Are you utilizing your opportunities to gather for beauty? Do you have a group of friends that you engage in this with? How often? Do you see how this adds to your sense of femininity?

For more information on Building a Feminine Community, visit www.LotusProjectBook.com

Self-Love

I have shared my take on life as a living yoga. Any way we can call in consciousness, deliciousness, gratitude, a good feeling as we go through the day is a way to engage in life positively. In the midst of the shifting world, we have tasks of self-care that we can enjoy and luxuriate in each day. This is self-love. Showering, getting dressed, using artistry in how we present ourselves. We have daily opportunities to nourish ourselves through these activities. We enjoy adornments and sparkles, good scents, tasty things that engage our senses. Each day you can enjoy the practice of honoring yourself.

Different colors, styles, matching jewelry and bangly bracelets engage our changing nature. Feeling good about the care and time you took to prepare yourself is a practice in deeper beauty. It shows that you honor yourself and take time to add pizzazz in your busy life. These acts of self-care and self-love are two important ingredients in beauty. Beauty is an honor you give to something. Give it to yourself!

You can use your heart and your feeling nature while doing these things—washing your face with scented ingredients of top quality, applying coconut oil slowly, remembering your body and how it carries you through the world as you nourish your skin, slowing down to do small acts of honor to yourself as you go through your day. Essential oils, fresh flowers, and sensual delights are the things of beauty to a woman. Preparing good, nourishing food, sharing things that you no longer need, deeply connecting to others in an open way. Finding practices and tools that relax you, give you safety, make you feel good and help you move forward—this is self-care. Take time to develop and tap into your feeling nature.

To see beautiful is to be beautiful, so look around for beauty. Let others see problems; find beauty wherever you can. It is a practice and it can be a habit. When you see more beauty, you are more beautiful. You see the reflection and strengthen it in your own nature. It is natural for you to see beauty for you are a woman. We beautify spaces, people, homes and meals. Relish the artistry of creating more beauty in and around your world.

Sink in to your essence and feel the beauty in yourself and others. This is sacred femininity. Treat yourself as sacred. Understand how that word feels to you. It is different for each of us but it is the deep feeling you are looking for—the love of yourself exactly as you are. We begin by finding joy in ourselves and honoring what is here right now. Beauty unfolds from within you through these practices.

Joyful Movement

To be healthful, to have a body that is fit, we need to move. Movement circulates oxygen, helps manage energy and stress, and creates endorphins that naturally make you feel good. Joyful movement, fitness, and exercise are part of beauty. When you connect to your body, when you feel good about how it moves, you honor yourself in a healthful way.

It is best if this movement is fun and you look forward to it. It should be something you really like that involves your emotions and your physical body but stops your mental chatter. Most people create a workout routine that is hard, one that pushes their limits and stresses them. They have to do it a certain way every time, and they constantly criticize themselves in their movements. This is not joyful and although it may help them become physically fit, doing it in stress and adrenaline undermines the feminine way.

My idea of joyful movement is dancing! Women should dance every day to develop their beauty. It is the most electrifying joy vibe a woman can generate mentally, physically, emotionally, and spiritually.

A dancing practice is described in Part Two of this book. The practice of free-form dancing will transform your physical being. By allowing your unique body to flow as it will, remembering your flexible feminine nature, releasing the rigidity of masculine energy, you can sink into your body. Dancing raises your pulse rate, increases oxygen intake and releases you from habitual thinking. We just dance and it is youthful and joyful. Yogis say it grounds us to the earth, balances our root chakra, mulahadara.

Reminding yourself of the feeling you get from joyous dancing creates a habit of remembering pleasure. Dancing energetically each day mixes up your magnetic field quickly and reclaims energy in your space. You swirl it back in for use. The lower vibrations can move out as you dance, so you can reclaim pleasure and oxytocin.

It is magical the wonder the universe offers when you go out in the world as a woman filled with joy and beauty. You are welcomed in a whole different way. You have a high vibration. Relaxed, feeling beautiful and full of your magnificence, you can go out into the world to share your gifts. The practice of dancing is a prayer, an honoring of the female body and it creates a magnetic field of love and protection around you.

Joyous movement creates beauty. It brings joy, freedom, happiness, even giddiness. It oxygenates your body and gets your heart flowing with vital energy, allowing you to smile and feel alive and magnetizing. This is why dance is so healthful to a woman's body.

We are different than men in many ways physically. Our bodies need different movements for health. Chinese medicine, Ayurvedic medicine, Egyptian movements—these ancient feminine cultures treated women's bodies differently and knew what made them thrive. Flowing movements, charming ways, and playful activities awaken our creativity. These involve different systems than the activities that strengthen men.

How did we miss this? What builds a man's body and physique is different than what builds a woman's body. Find out about yourself, learn how to produce joy in movement. This will create more health for you than following a routine designed for others. The expressive arts are part of our fabric as woman, these offer us different types of movements.

Dancing will lead the way. I have never met a woman who didn't like dancing! In fact, when I tell women that dancing is the best way to reconnect with their bodies and create health, they all smile so big. Is it that easy? Indeed it is! The secret is that we love to do it. Ladies, if you want more beauty, more magnetism, more allure, dance through life! And love yourself exactly as you are.

The Lotus Bloom

So here we are, lovely women in the process of blooming. Yes, the muck and mire is all around us and we are deeply rooted in it. We naturally shoot forth our stem through the water, rising up towards the sun. When we see ourselves as lovely flowers, queens of beauty, majestic gifts learning to unfold, we find joy within.

I want to bloom like the pure white lotus! Rising up through the water, finding my place, standing tall in the pond, holding steadily at the root, my essence grounded in my body, I flow in the water, bud, and bloom. When I open I am a glorious, scented flower that inspires the highest in spirit. Everything around me delights in me. I am part of the great pond, holding my place in magnificence.

Together we can honor ourselves this way and give ourselves great power to intuit our way through life. We are in this pond together, swaying in the wind side by side. Let's claim this purpose in unison and strengthen our feminine way. Let us delight in ourselves and the role that we are called to bloom into. Blooming is not toiling and striving, it is just a matter of opening our buds of beauty.

Each of us is a Lotus Project. Growing forth like the lotus from the mud and heaviness of the Earth, shooting our stems up to begin our bloom, our cyclical journey. We are becoming with or without consciousness. We are in a moving world that evolves toward goodness innately. We create our lives about us in an artistic way when we feel our way through.

You tap into this creative essence, the root of your being, through playful experience. You open up. You stroke the brush with grace and loveliness. Our hearts know the way, our intuition is strong, our sensitivity is growing and the canvas is before us. Bloom we will! Do so with the understanding that we are creators. To know this deeply and move from our feeling center makes life such a pleasure. It inspires us, motivates us, and gives us passion to go forward.

It is time for us to bloom in sweet magnificence, choosing daily practices that shift us to a more heartfelt level. Engaging more lovingly in all that we do, slowing down to smell the roses, sharing a cup of tea, beautifying

Lyn Hicks

ourselves as we prepare to face and nurture the world using our flowing way. These are the self-nourishing ways that make for a wonderful bloom—honoring the unfolding, relishing it, enjoying your emotional nature, understanding that this is your gift, your intuitive way to feel the world. This turns living into an art.

Use the tools in this book to reawaken your artistry, your heartfelt nature and your ability to honor yourself and others through your choices. These pages offer many techniques and perspectives that can create a powerful shift within you, enabling you to enjoy life more. They are practical tools to engage your awareness of who you are. Find other women to gather with and use the power of your community to institute these practices in your lives.

We are creating this new way together to bring balance to the world. It has not existed yet in this modern time when women truly value themselves and their brilliance. Awaken your feminine essence by choosing to honor yourself, others and the wonder of your femininity. Doing this together we will build the way and create a stronger, more caring community for all.

We deserve to be heard, to be powerful, to nourish the world with our gifts. Nature is our ally and our guide. Relax into yourself! You are already a flower and now you will step into your magnificent bloom. It is our time and in unison we will create a magical place to live. Pure white lotuses we are, opening and releasing our fragrance to the world! Beauty is our form! We are the expression of sacred femininity, the flowers of our world!

Part Two
Practices in Vitality

This part of the book includes specific kinds of movement practices that offer multiple benefits. They are simple and brief; this is not an hour of working out. These are movements that will nourish you, raise your energy, and teach you to manage it and include your heart, mind and body in unison.

These practices will transform you. I invite you to do them often. They are called practices because they are meant to be done regularly. You can practice raising your emotional level and your vital energy. You must use movement and understand your energy by learning to feel it and recognizing the emotions that run you. Aharaj yoga is about managing your emotions for your own purposes—it teaches you about the energy of your emotions, the power they have to move you or hold you down.

This is a feeling universe. It is not all about thinking. Ideas in the head and ideas with emotion are quite different; ultimately you blend the two. These practices come from ancient traditions based on principles of yoga, Ayurvedic medicine and health. I am so proud to share this information with you as you grow to live vibrantly! Enjoy!

The Breath of Passion

In many circles, the breath is considered the gift of life. When you stop breathing, you stop being alive. There are so many great teachings on breathing that are worth investigating. I am offering you a simple yet powerful way to use your breath to connect with your pleasure. The goal is to create oxytocin in your system.

Oxytocin is a hormone that comes into play during childbirth, breastfeeding, and when we give birth and when we get pleasure from sex. It creates a relaxed state in which we feel safe, calm and nurtured. If you are anxious when you breastfeed, you can't release your milk properly.

Women's hormone is oxytocin when we are in the states that feel safest, most pleasurable, even orgasmic. It is part of the parasympathetic nervous system which is the biochemical pathway where females thrive. When we are operating in ease, we feel safe, strong, and relaxed and are then able to create our greatest work.

The male-oriented business world pushes us to use our adrenal systems because the economy is based on a competitive model. It is important to use masculine traits sometimes but women who do this too often end up in a state of stress, feeling tired, cranky, and uninspired. We are creators so we like to feel safe and connected, flowing gracefully and enjoying it.

Pleasure! This is a function of the parasympathetic nervous system. It is not just thinking we are okay, but feeling deeply relaxed, a calm intensity in all of our being. It is beyond the sigh; it is the pleasure state of the body and its systems. When you are in it you know it. Most of the time we are not, at least not fully. When this state becomes our way of being, we will flourish and flower.

This breathing exercise will transform you. Practicing it, you will feel this oxytocin state and you will feel your heart open. You will begin to notice the difference between when you are feeling relaxed and safe and when you are in adrenaline. It will get deeper and you can use this breathing practice to help you gain awareness of when your feminine essence is operating.

There are many ways to do this breathing and you will begin to sense when you shift into the parasympathetic nervous system. Trust yourself and your own way. I learned it from my Sacred Femininity study called the Breath of Passion. Ellie Drake, founder of BraveHeart Women, teaches it in a special way. You can find her online and she offers much wisdom from a doctor's point of view. She calls it the Oxytocin Breath. You want to use some form of this breathing throughout your day until being in the oxytocin space becomes a habit.

This practice is all about the exhale, how you release the breath. Exhale first. The inhale should just allow the next breath to come in; it is not an aggressive suck in of air. It is an allowing of the breath that fills your belly and then a long deep exhale with a pleasurable sound and smile. It is so delicious that it gives you this sound feeling of pleasure. We use the sounds *Aaaah*, *Ooooh*, or *Mmmm*, in the Breath of Passion. They sound sexual, and we are not used to making these sounds out loud.

You can practice deep breathing and feel your body switch to the parasympathetic system, relaxed in safety and pleasure. It will take some doing it but you will feel the change in the vibration of your body. Remember that these energy shifts are subtle and you must increase your perception to feel them. The goal is to retrain the body to move into this state with a simple adjustment of your breath, noticing when you need to re-center. This is also using the nutrition of oxygen. Conscious, relaxed breathing nourishes all of your body with oxygen.

The Practice

Sit in a relaxed position with your shoulders, face, and body relaxed, taking a moment to check in with yourself. Allow the inbreath in the belly to fill you. Once you are ready to exhale, release the breath with the *Aaaaaah*, *Oooooh*, or *Mmmmmm* sound. Make sure it is long, strong, and has a pleasurable sound so your body can hear as well as feel this state.

When this is done right, you may feel a tingling in your head as the hypothalamus tells your body to shift into the parasympathetic pathway. Each of us is different in how we experience our bodies and this shift. Find your place with it. Practice it many times and see if you notice when the shift happens. Your body will tingle in relaxation! To me it feels like bubbles oozing through my body. It is very wonderful and pleasurable. It is worth mastering this and understanding how you feel in relaxation.

Mmmm is the easiest sound to start with because we are familiar with that sound when we eat something scrumptious. The pleasure center in the womb is also tied to the sense of taste. When something is delicious, we activate oxytocin when we appreciate the flavor and goodness of it. In this practice you are doing it without the food, relearning how to consciously shift your vibration into relaxed pleasure through breathing.

I constantly use this throughout my day, even in my car, making these sounds regularly to train myself to feel that openness. I was rarely in it so it has been a great tip for me. As you practice this breath throughout the day, you begin to have power over your state of being. This breath allows you to quickly switch systems and move into a more creative feminine energy. Practice this often, taking many breaths in each sitting. Notice your body and state and you can learn to create more pleasurable moments in your days.

We all have our own sounds. These basic pleasure sounds allow us to learn how breath, voice and sound can relax us immediately. Find your own way with it. Create your own sounds that feel good and induce a pleasurable vibe that reminds you that you are relaxing into your body and your life. Ground into the present and the calmness of your body.

Conscious Eating

This is an exercise and teaching I learned from Joshua Duncan's Aharaj yoga teachers. There should be a great joy in eating and most of us just overlook it. We forget and we miss out on the levels of nourishment we could be getting.

Whenever we do anything, we do it physically, mentally, spiritually and emotionally. We may not realize that all these aspects are getting recorded but they are. Often when we eat, we are doing a number of other things at the same time. We could be on the run, watching the news, having a conversation or even a disagreement. We could be eating because we are emotionally low or overeating while celebrating. We eat in many ways for many purposes.

Conscious eating is about realizing that when you take in food, you are taking in emotions and thinking as well. As that food becomes part of your cells, so do all the emotions and thoughts. They become part of your being as they move through your body.

All levels of you are happening at once. Once you realize this, you can make your nourishing more powerful and healthful by consciously being in a better state when you eat. It is great that we say grace for our food, and sometimes even think with gratitude about all the processes that go into creating our meal. Conscious eating goes a step further and adds a lot to your vitality and nourishment. Eating in this way will make you a stronger, more focused being. Practice it once a day or whenever you remember, ideally at every meal.

The Practice

Take a moment to honor your food by saying grace or following whatever custom you prefer. This begins to put you in a relaxed state of gratitude which helps your digestion.

As you eat each bit, think of the positive intentions you have for life and the good things that are going on. Eat with positive conversation. Think of your dreams, your goals, your projects and your current endeavors as you eat. This attaches your good intentions to your food. Your mind is positive, your emotions are strong and hopeful.

Enjoy your food as well. Taste it, notice the flavor and texture and the unrushed pleasure of truly being nourished by the act of eating. Take in

Lyn Hicks

the pleasure of the food, the taste, the emotion of joy, the power of your intentions.

Continue to eat in joy with these ideas in your head. These feelings and thoughts go into your cells as the nourishing food does. Your physical body now has these things programmed in. You are nourished on all levels. You enjoy your meal immensely and now you can go about your day knowing these intentions are literally part of you.

Your basic body will do its best to bring them about because they are part of your being now. Conscious nourishment on all levels will change your very health and vitality profoundly. This beautiful practice will build your joy and well-being!

Dancing with Your Spirit

Women's power is in their hips, the svadisthana chakra, where the womb is located. Deepak Chopra calls this the self's dwelling place. The kidneys are in this area and in Chinese medicine they provide vitality and youth.

Women have many physical problems in this area such as fibroids, heavy painful cycles and even infertility. This is because we are cut off from the real power that resides there. It is stuck, stopped and used only for men when it is meant to be used in all our systems to awaken our greatness. It is sexual, creative energy. It is where the masculine and feminine energy of creation commingle. The vagus nerve, the messenger to the hypothalamus, starts here in our belly. Our hips are our base of flexibility; the way we relate to others comes from this energy center in yoga traditions.

We live in our heads too much! We may as well have cartoon bubbles floating above us. Our physical bodies are busy at some task, our hearts are somewhere else, our wholeness is scattered and unaligned. This exercise is designed to ground you back into your beautiful body. Dancing in joy with your hips, your individual grace, your heart in oxytocin and pleasure, your expression open and beautiful, awakens a state of joy that changes your entire being and energy field. Doing this reinforces the oxytocin state, the state we as women should be moving in throughout life, releasing us from the "fight or flight" mode of the sympathetic nervous system.

This practice incorporates feminine movement. It calls in joy through your heart, creating a great feeling of bliss and beauty like a prayer. It clears stagnant energy in your body, transforming it through movement in joy. It creates oxytocin and activates the parasympathetic nervous system, putting you into "tend and befriend" mode through dancing. It allows you to relax all your bodies in safety, bringing your biochemistry into a state that is optimal for creating.

This is a powerful practice! Doing it every day will remind you how it feels to be in the biochemical state of relaxation that will allow you to thrive. This is simple and fun movement for women. Our empowerment comes from this pleasurable, joyous state that is natural to our bodies.

It is easy to connect to our femininity, for we are women. It is not hard; it's not something that we "have to" do. The greatest thing about these feminine practices is that they are fun, natural and easy. Dancing is the perfect example of how simple it can be to connect with ourselves and our feminine ways.

The Practice

Begin by playing music—whatever you like, whatever makes your heart sing, makes you smile and fills you with joy. This dance is not for anyone else. It's just for you!

Settle into your body. Let it move how it wants to—gracefully, sensually, with ease and beauty. Touch your body with your hands of love. Feel your hair, your shoulders, your face, your throat, arms, legs, all of you. Touch your body with the fronts and backs of your hands, the way you would want someone to touch you with softness and gentleness. Feel grounded, feel the earth underneath your feet. Let the body move how it wants to without thinking.

Feel love for this basic self of yours. Love this body that runs your heart, your digestive system, all the functions that happen every day without conscious effort. Send love and gratitude to yourself. Give yourself the love and gratitude that you seek from others and feel it for yourself. Feel pleasure and joy for having this body, for how it has carried you through life with all its beauty and magnificence. You are blessed to be alive, to have breath, to have this wonderful body.

Do this for at least 15 minutes so you can get out of your head and clear the thoughts about what you "should be" doing. Close your eyes and you can enter a trancelike state, blending with the music, doing just what you are doing. Stay long enough to feel great love and joy in just dancing as a woman, full of love and grace. No thoughts, no negative judgments, just the joy of being in all your fullness.

Dance like no one is watching! Generate feelings of love and joy for yourself and others. Allow your body to move how it wants and needs to, not thinking but letting its wisdom take over in movement. Some days I feel graceful, other days my body is almost spastic. Allow the wisdom of your body to guide your movement while your heart opens in joy and breathing, your mind happy and flowing with the fun of what you are doing.

When you are done, notice how you feel. How is your energy? How radiant do you feel? Do you feel confident? Pleased? Ready to begin the day with joy and openness? What resistance did you feel? What areas of your body were hard to love? What feelings came up as you gave love to yourself?

This experience offers great wisdom. I know when I began it seemed kind of silly but I just went through it as a practice and watched what feelings arose as I tried to just be with myself in all my magnificence. I was shocked at how I wanted to stop, at how childish I felt. Why couldn't I just be with myself in pleasure and wonder, feeling joyful about this body I travel in? I saw the wisdom in getting beyond my initial reservations.

Three Dances

You can dance in your own unique way for this practice, so there is no "The Practice" section describing the movements. I offer thoughts below on how to approach these dances. Make them your own!

You can start by doing this practice in the shower as you prepare for your day. I suggest dancing to three songs a day. The first dance is for the Light, God, the Creator, the Great Mind, the Source. Dance in gratitude for the gift of life, of being able to move and create on the Earth. I dance to the Light that I am part of, that is in me, that animates me. Doing this can conjure the joy of being alive as you move.

The next dance shows gratitude for all those who have taught you great wisdom, for the teachers of all sorts who have helped you grow and become who you are. As I dance, I think of being totally sustained by the Earth as well as all the teachers, teachings, and knowledge I have encountered that have helped me become who I am. Knowing that I am supported, I can feel that I am part of a greater "we". All the ideas and communities I am part of encourage me to bring forth my greatest expression and I can tap into their group energy. This dance can help you feel supported and grateful, perfect where you are in life and learning.

In the third dance, you take all the gratitude, love, support, generosity, and joy you just generated and send it out to others. Send it to your family, friends, and community, then expand it to those in crisis. Try expanding it further, generating and sending love to the whole world. A very powerful workout!

This dancing practice will connect you with your Shakti power, the creative energy in your hips. It will increase your magnetism, helping you attract what you want in life. You will feel more open and beautiful, more playful and inspired. It will remind you what the high state of joy feels like as it pulsates through your body, spirit and heart.

So enjoy this practice! It has been done for thousands of years in the hidden tents of women in ancient cultures. It will joyfully expand you and awaken you to a new energy that can be your greatest asset. Once you remember and reinforce this state through dancing, I have no doubt that you will be able to call it up from many other things in your life that inspire you. This practice reminds you where your power as a woman resides. Dance through life, ladies!

Chakra Clearing

The practice of chakra clearing will help you begin to understand your energy field. It offers you a way back to awareness of the moment with clarity and peace. The seven chakras are located in seven specific places along the center of your body. They are energy centers, each one representing a different kind of energy we use in our lives. Consciously focusing on these areas, adding new energy and breaking up old energy stirs up your body's energy field, allowing movement. You will notice the clarity that chakra clearing brings.

Aharaj yoga is a wonderful practice that works with all your chakras. It is simple and effective at shifting your state and enhancing your clarity. Aharaj yoga is called the yoga of empowerment. You will use your emotions, your mental focus and your movements in unison to align and shift you in all your bodies. When doing the moves, focus on these areas to make the practice more effective.

Know that as you do this practice, you are adding new energy and clearing stagnant beliefs and blocks. Emotionally feel relaxed but powerful. You control your emotional state; you are in charge of all your bodies. Physically do the moves in strength and see if you can sense the invisible energy in your chakras. This energy is subtle so you have to tune your awareness to it. Some sense it at first, others notice over time. Aharajyoga. com provides information about this special kind of yoga and Joshua Duncan's website (joshuaduncan.net) is a good resource for learning about this practice.

The Practice

Begin by standing with your feet at shoulder width. Notice how you feel. What is your state? Happy, tired, annoyed?

You will do two movements two times for each chakra. The first movement will be rubbing your hands together to create heat and new energy. Massage practitioners often do this before they begin and Reiki masters do it to activate the healing energy from their hands. Your hands offer your gifts to the world so they are important instruments of your body.

The second movement is clapping your hands together to break up any energy that is stuck in your field. Do each movement for a short time, say 10 or 15 seconds. The last movement will be expanding your hands out and away to your sides after clapping the second time. This expands the new energy you added and the old energy you broke up, allowing newness into your field.

Rub your hands together with your fingertips pointing upward just above the top of your head at the crown chakra, called the Sahaswara. Rub your hands for a few moments, then clap them, rub your hands then clap, now expand the energy by moving your arms out and down to your sides. This chakra is your connection to the source, the highest good of all, and this practice opens your universal connection.

Your Ajna chakra is between your eyes at the bridge of your nose. Rub your hands, then clap, rub then clap, then expand the energy outward. This expands your focus, your big plan, the blueprint of your ideas. It is the energy you use to remain focused on your purpose, keeping your eye on the goal you are working toward.

Your Vishuddha chakra is in your throat and neck area. This is the place of individuality, creativity, and personal expression. Rub then clap, removing the old voices that hold you back. Rub then clap. Now expand your arms out to your sides, expanding your voice, your unique expression of yourself.

Your Anahata chakra is located at your heart. Many negative emotions such as guilt, shame, and unworthiness reside here. Rub then clap, rub then clap to break up the negative energy. Extend your hands and feel the unconditional love expand about you.

Your Manipura chakra is located at your navel. Here, your fingertips are to point forward as you rub and clap. This is the area of action, of business, of making things happen. Your vital life energy is here. Rub for new energy, clap out laziness and lethargic tendencies, rub and clap. Now expand the field of action, expand your power to do the appropriate things to enhance your life.

Your Svadisthana chakra is at your belly, below your navel. This is the area that controls flexibility in communication, in relationships, in life. Point your fingertips down as you clear this area. Rub and clap, rub and clap, then expand your flexibility and adaptability. Clearing this chakra will help you flow more easily through life.

Finally, put your hands behind you at the tailbone with fingers pointed down. This is the Muladhara chakra, which regulates your physical body, your stability, your ability to bring down whatever you want to manifest. It is your connection to physicality and it controls health. Rub and clap, rub and clap, now expand your health, your strong stance and your ability to create what you desire.

Now that you have worked with each chakra, take two cleansing breaths. Your hands circle up above your head and then, as you move them down your center along your spine, you do seven sharp exhales, one at each chakra. Make a shew sound as you exhale. Your hands are like a level as you shew your breath out down the front of your body. This brings the new energy into your spine at each chakra.

Do two sets of seven exhales then just notice how you feel compared to when you started. This is a wonderful practice to keep your energy high and bring clarity and awareness to your day if you are physically or mentally tired.

Lyn Hicks

Releasing Exercise

Aharaj yoga works with energy. It uses the Manipura chakra at your solar plexus—the energy of fire, digestion, and transformation—to clear your system. This is our power center of action. When you do the movements it is important to remember you are tapping into this emotional, burning energy of fury. You are using this energy for change and your thinking when using this energy is powerful and strong like a warrior's.

You are using your power to clear your state and you will use your voice to express your strong energy. Haaa with power is the sound you make as you do this. When you move physically, you are strong and vital. You are full of force to clear your system of unwanted negative energy. So you are powerfully transforming, releasing your block and your annoyance in strength, sound and fury.

The Practice

Stand with your feet shoulder-width apart. Cross your arms as you put your fists in front of your shoulders, making an X over your chest. Powerfully, with emotion and the sound ha, jump and straighten your arms to your sides. Do this ten times with force, power and a feeling of being in control of your clearing.

Now take a cleansing breath and notice how you feel. Do you feel more aware, alert and vital? Do you feel your clarity?

This is the most powerful move for shifting your energy field and getting out of your head, out of annoyance, anxiety, stress, and anger. It takes the angst in your body and expresses it using all your bodies—mental, physical and emotional. It transforms the tension so it is no longer circling in you. It is out and expressed in a controlled manner.

You are clearer now, able to move ahead without that nervous energy. Practicing this expression of negativity, of the stress that comes about just from being alive, helps us to be more stable in general. The effect is like cleaning out your emotional energy so it doesn't build up and spill out on someone. It also teaches us to control this powerful energy by releasing it in a productive way.

We can also use it as a positive force to move forward from a starting point of commitment: "I am going to do this no matter what. Nothing will stop me; I am a powerful creator of good things." The more challenging and stressful emotions provide us power to clear and build anew. As we practice noticing and clearing our anxiety we begin to understand this vital energy and how to use it wisely for our purposes. Try it and see what happens!

The Goddess Glow
(Movements for Health, Beauty and Grace)

Women need to learn to move all the parts of their torsos. All our organs are housed there and moving these areas brings great flexibility and health. Movement allows for any stuck or stagnant energy to be released and travel out.

Women can increase their health through graceful body movements. Women are disconnected from their bodies, ungrounded in them. We have forgotten our beautiful way. Connecting to our beauty, our sensuality and our grace enhances health and vitality. The moves of this practice can fit in your day while you are on the phone or doing the dishes, anywhere that you will have a few minutes on your feet. As you make the movements, stay aware of the area you are moving to create more effect.

The Practice

Start by rolling your head from side to side. This allows you to get out of your thinking mind and release the neck tension that almost everyone carries. Do each movement at least 15 times. Listen to your body to determine whether to do more.

Roll your shoulders forward many times, then backward. Do this each way as many times as you feel necessary. Allow your body to dictate; it will increase your connection to yourself.

Hold your breasts for a moment and remember they are yours! Realize that the milk of life comes from them and your nourishing heart lies behind this powerful area of your body. Move them forward then backward. Feel the release as you gain mobility here.

Now move your ribs from side to side. You can put your arms out if it helps. Bend your knees so you are isolating your ribs. This is a challenging move but we need to allow movement here.

Move your breasts and ribs forward, side, back and side, and repeat a few times. Then move this area in a circle. Now move in a circle the other way. This opens your heart and begins circulation and release in this area.

Move your hips from side to side many times. Move your hips from front to back many times. Now circle your hips one way several times. Then circle them the other way. Be sure to isolate the motion so it is all in your hips.

Now do figure eights with your hips—both ways. Bring your feet together and do the figure eights again.

Do slow Kegel exercises, slowly tightening your vaginal muscle to a count of five, like you are raising a ball to your belly button in slow motion. Relax. Do five repetitions. Movement here is very important for urinary and reproductive health.

Gyrate your legs as you relax your upper body. Do this for at least two minutes until you feel a nice release in your body.

CONCLUSION

These practices are great for warming up, dancing, or just putting a little movement in your day to connect to your grace in movement. Put a smile on your face as you do these, remembering they are building a connection to your glorious beauty and increasing your health on many levels. Adding a state of joy to things allows oxytocin to be released so it can de-stress your body. You are a lovely woman and honoring yourself begins within!

Recommended Resources

Local Resources

Terree Yeagle is an Eastern Pennsylvania based photographer and owner of The Moment Photography. Her studio specializes in capturing the milestones of human life with a sense of wonder and romance. In addition to her work with people Terree has begun a line of decorative photographs called Harvest Capture Designs, capturing the essence of the natural world. She can be found at TheMomentPhoto.com

Dr. Lauren Nappen
Chiropractic, Reiki, Aromatherapy, and more
www.ahhhjustingtolife.com

Blooming Glen Farm
Community Supported Agriculture
www.BloomingGlenFarm.com

Green Collaboration
Bucks County Green Business Networking, Events, and Blog
www.greencollaboration.org

Environmental Home Cleaning
www.harmonyclean.com

Valerie Hopkins
Drum Circles
www.drumcirclesheal.com

Diane Wing, M.A.
Author, teacher, personal transformation guide, and intuitive consultant
www.DianeWing.com

Rosie Jones, Hair By Rosie
215-794-3589

Bucks County Wellness
www.buckscountywellnesscentre.com

Authors

Deepak Chopra, M.D.

Louise Hay

Mother Maya (Maya Tiwari)

Christiane Northrop, M.D.

John-Roger, DSS

Suggested Reading

Spiritual Health and Wellness, by John Roger DDS

The Four Agreements, by don Miguel Ruiz

A New Earth: Awakening to Your Life's Purpose, by Eckhart Tolle

Wishing You, by Dr. Lauren Nappen

When the Drummers Were Women, by Layne Redmond

Women's Power to Heal Through Inner Medicine, by Sri Swamini Mayatitananda (Maya Tiwari)

Online Resources

www.aharajyoga.com
Aharaj yoga resource

www.msia.org
The Movement of Spiritual Inner Awareness

www.harmonyhillgardens.com
My eco-conscious farm, venue for gatherings, classes and growing flowers!

www.melaleuca.com
Environmental home products

www.mountainroseherbs.com
Organic herbs, spices and essential oils

www.ab-editing.com
Environmentally friendly editing, proofreading and writing

www.TheAuthorIncubator.com
The Author Incubator & The Difference Press
Book publishing for life coaches

ABOUT THE AUTHOR

Lyn Hicks is a practical educator of health, wellbeing and green living for a thriving life of vitality. She is trained in the oral tradition of Dragon Gate Tia Chi Chuan, Raja Yoga from the Northern Gate of the Himalayans and Sacred Femininity of Ancient Cultures through traveling masters at retreats on her farm. She offers simple easy ways to connect with your body for health awareness, working to activate and support the body's natural intelligence and awaken the intuition.

She shares her yoga of living on her organic flower farm in Pennsylvania. A love of nature, beauty and grace inspires Lyn to share the power of feminine essence with other woman. After doing this herself, it became natural to share with others through writing, videos and classes and retreats at her farm. Her passion is to use collaborative feminine power to strengthen and to change the world into a more nourished placed.

Passionate about health and wellness, nature, spirituality and alternative medicine, Lyn has found great learning and healing in this life study. Through her own efforts to seek the simplest, easiest health and vitality movements to promote a sound body for herself, she has learned great wisdom and continues in this.

Lyn

Lyn Hicks
lyn@harmonyhillgardens.com
215-997-5005

Her current projects include:

- Public Speaker for the Feminine, Green, and Local Movements
- Author of The Lotus Project, Alluring Well-being and Beauty through Green Living
- Lotus Project at Harmony Hill Gardens Organic Flower Farm: Host and educator of health/wellness and feminine empowerment. www.harmonyhillgardens.com
- The Green Collaboration, a community of Green Business in Bucks County, PA.: Cofounder and Organizer. www.greencollaboration.org
- Independent Wellness and Educator: Offering a variety of Wellness and Feminine Empowerment courses to the community for hire.
- Harmony Hill Gardens: Organic Flower Grower, Floral Designer, Specialty Floral Event Designer www.harmonyhillgardens.com
- White Lotus Cottage: A destination offering a garden of healing practitioners. www.whitelotuscottage.com

You can find out more about her philosophy and perspective through her blog. www.harmonyhillgardens.blogspot.com